THE
ULTIMATE
LOW-CARB
PLAN

The Last Diet Book You'll Ever Buy

By William Barnhill

American Media, Inc.

THE ULTIMATE LOW-CARB PLAN
The Last Diet Book You'll Ever Buy

Copyright © 2004 AMI Books, Inc.
Cover design: Carlos Plaza
Interior design: Debbie Browning

ISBN: 1-932270-41-8

First printing: October 2004
Printed in the United States of America

10 9 8 7 6 5 4 3 2 1

DEDICATION

A special thanks to a special consultant, Wendy Arthur, M.D., director of complementary and holistic healthcare at Clayton College of Natural Health, whose wisdom and expert counsel made The Ultimate Low-Carb Plan *a reality.*

This book provides general information about an important subject but it is not a substitute for the individual diagnosis and prescriptions that only your doctor can provide. You must use common sense in applying this information to your own situation. You should have a complete physical (including appropriate lab tests) before starting any diet or exercise program. Get your doctor's approval before starting any diet or exercise program and if your doctor doesn't approve, don't start.

TABLE OF CONTENTS

Losing The Battle   9
What's It All About?   18
A Bite Of Dr. Atkins   25
Myths & Misinformation   30
In The Zone – Diet Of The Stars   36
Flush Your Fat Away   43
The South Beach Diet   53
Your Ultimate Low-Carb Plan   58
Let's Eat   63
Turning Back Snack Attacks   142
Away From Home   148
Moving Your Fat Away   152
Counting C's   161
Making It Easier   270
Find It Online   327

CHAPTER 1

LOSING THE BATTLE

Americans have been fighting the battle of the bulge for decades — and tens of millions of us are losing. Are YOU one of those? Probably, if you're reading this book. So read on and learn how you can become a winner.

Obesity has reached epidemic proportions in this country, so much so that the U.S. Surgeon General and other health authorities have declared weight control a national priority.

Americans now consume an average of 2,000 calories a day, up from 1,800 in the 1970s, according to one survey by the Calorie Control Council. Considering most health authorities believe that a woman can thrive on 1,500 and a man on 1,500 to 1,800, is it any wonder obesity is epidemic?

According to the National Health and Nutrition Examination Survey (NHANES), nearly 65 percent of adult Americans are overweight, 33 percent are obese — and many seem to have abandoned their weight-loss efforts because of reported failure to reach unreasonable goal weights, reveals the American Dietetic Association.

Obesity-related medical conditions are the second leading cause of death in America (after smoking-related illnesses), resulting in 300,000 lives lost each year and an estimated health-care tab of $70 billion.

At any given time about 25 percent of American men and 45 percent of women are trying to lose weight. Scores of diet plans — each promising great, fast and permanent weight loss — have been developed. Some of them work for a time, but are complicated and difficult to follow. Others are just plain boring, so low in fats and the things we all love to eat, many dieters abandon them.

Still others are unhealthy fad diets, calling for use of bizarre quack products to "melt" fat or block it from developing. Desperate dieters try them all the same. Far too often, these diets fail; weight is lost, then re-gained, in what health authorities have come to call "the yo-yo syndrome" — up and down, up and down.

Nearly 30 years ago, heart specialist Robert Atkins, M.D., launched a revolutionary movement — controlling weight by cutting back on fattening carbohydrates. His concept flew in the face of America's nutritional establishment, which made him a prime target for those promoting diets that restrict fat, but allow dieters to eat all the carbs they want.

Their complaints, often coming from the commercial groups being hardest hit by the movement toward low-carb dining, have become increasingly strident; low-carb diets, it would seem, can cause everything from infertility to warts. But they offer little hard science to support their allegations.

Meanwhile, Americans, discovering the effectiveness of the low-carb program, have largely ignored the critics. Today, according to one recent survey, some 26 million Americans are following strict low-carb regimens and 70 million more restrict their carb intake.

As the low-carb lifestyle grew from a mere trickle in the '70s to a raging torrent today, science has begun catching up — and coming down on the side of low-carb dieting. During the first half of 2004 alone, stunning results were published by scientists at the prestigious University of Pennsylvania and Duke University.

Both showed dieters lose more unwanted fat on low-carb diets than on low-fat diets — and they lose it faster. What's more, the researchers found that those on low-carb diets had higher levels of "good" cholesterol and levels of "bad" cholesterol about the same as those on low-fat diets. Even though they consumed far more fats, they had far lower levels of triglycerides. In one study, low-carb dieters reduced triglyceride levels by an astounding 49 percent. That's pretty impressive!

And while we're speaking of science, in early August 2004, researchers, including one from the Harvard School of Public Health, reported that women who eat diets high in carbs are more than twice as likely to get breast cancer as those who restrict their intake of sugar and starch. In a report in the journal *Cancer Epidemiology, Biomarkers and Prevention*, the researchers speculate that carbohydrates may increase the risk of breast cancer by triggering a heavy release of insulin, which causes cells to divide rapidly, stimulating high levels of estrogen — which can encourage breast cancer.

Wendy Arthur, M.D., director of complementary and holistic healthcare at Clayton College in Birmingham, Alabama, was asked for her medical opinion of the top low-carb diets — and of *The Ultimate Low-Carb Plan*. Here's what she said:

"For those 70 percent of Americans who are overweight and/or have elevated cholesterol, triglycerides and blood sugar, these diets have a moderate to excellent chance of reducing your weight and possibly your risk for heart disease and strokes.

"The granddaddy of high-protein diets is the **Atkins Diet**. The men in the family who are meat lovers and do not have renal disease will be able to follow it, even on the road. For short term, the weight comes off quickly, but some individuals have a hard time with staying in ketosis. For individuals wanting convenience there are bountiful Atkins products in grocery and convenience stores.

"Any individual who stays on a high-protein diet long term should have his or her kidney function checked, drink plenty of water and consider consuming only organic or natural meat/poultry as recommended by Ann Louise Gittleman, Ph.D., C.N.S.

"The merit of the **Fat Flush Plan** [see page 43] with these six diets is the unique detoxification in the phase 1 which can be repeated seasonally and/or for individuals with PMS/menstrual irregularity. She teaches the use of thermogenic herbs for seasoning. Gittleman also addresses the importance of organic foods. She discusses personalizing the program and adaptations for our multicultural nation. There are charts for protein to be adjusted based on individualized health needs. Some individuals with a distaste for cranberry juice and/or lemon may not be able to remain on the diet," states Dr. Arthur.

"The **Zone Diet** helps maintain our ratio of carbohydrate/protein/fat to 40/30/30. This zone assists in keeping insulin levels stable. Insulin resistance is an underlying culprit of many chronic diseases such as diabetes, polycystic ovary disease, increased risk of heart attacks, to name few. The merit of the diet are that it addresses multicultural aspects, children, exercise. Many of these diets are very difficult for vegetarians. However, this diet recommends soy as the major protein. Most studies suggest that soy consumption should be limited to several times a week as it interferes with thyroid and minerals in the body.

"The **South Beach Diet** merit is the emphasis in the use of healthy carbohydrates and fats after the low-carb Phase 1. The limiting factor is that the physician states no exercise is needed at a time when most Americans need at least one hour of walking per day minimum for health and stress reduction, as well as reducing the risk of osteoporosis," Dr. Arthur continues.

"The **Ultimate Low-Carb Plan**, as described in this book, is excellent. It takes dieters into their new lifestyles slowly and easily, without demanding immediate, radical changes in their dining habits or the foods they eat — one of the major causes for the infamous yo-yo syndrome.

"It is a plan for a new, more healthy lifestyle, rather than just a diet. The author asks his readers to get themselves moving by finding pleasant, enjoyable ways to step up their level of fitness and suggests ways they can improve their calorie burn dramatically by simple lifestyle activity changes.

"And his emphasis on using the Internet fits right into our 21st century electronic age, when there is a computer in nearly every home, and many homes have two or more," concludes Dr. Arthur.

Low-carb diets can have a downside, too. Restricting carbs too severely can lead to some problems, though they are easily correctable. Dehydration can occur. So can bad breath. Fatigue can be a problem for some, especially for athletes and those who do hard physical labor and need carbs for fast energy.

And for many, maintaining a low-carb diet is difficult because, though there are a multitude of commercial carb counters in the marketplace, they often disagree on carb counts for some foods.

The Ultimate Low-Carb Plan will show you how you can overcome or avoid those problems.

Just remember, though, no book can take the

place of sound medical advice from a physician you trust. So see your doctor before you start this or any other diet or exercise program and, by all means, carry this book with you.

So, where do we begin this marvelous new lifestyle? Well, how do you eat an elephant? The simple answer: one small bite at a time.

That's how *The Ultimate Low-Carb Plan* will lead you toward better health, more energy, better appearance and, of course, a trimmer, fitter and lighter body — one small bite at a time. We'll give you a bite of Atkins, the granddaddy of all low-carb diets, and a second bite straight out of The Zone. We'll flush a little fat with the Fat Flush Plan and take a walk down South Beach. These are all great diets, written by the stars of the nutritional world, and well worth reading.

The Ultimate Low-Carb Plan is a synthesis of all those, a way you can take a bite here and a bite there to formulate your own tailor-made dietary regimen ... the LAST one you will ever need for the rest of your life.

To help you make it work even better, we'll give you a sampling of exercises that will help burn off excess pounds at the same time they tone your muscles, bring you more energy and endurance, and (the icing on this low-carb cake) relieve stress. Lack of proper exercise is a major reason dieters don't lose.

Snacking is the second major barrier to weight loss. We'll tell you why and what to do about it. And you'll find some tips on scrumptious low-carb snacks you can use to take the place of potato chips and candy.

Later in this book, we'll be offering some particularly tasty low-carb recipes, a five-day sample low-carb menu that really works and a short carb counter from the Food and Nutrition Service at the U.S. Department of Agriculture, with directions to a vast storehouse of low-carb information, yours, free for the taking, on the Internet.

We'll tell you about some of the tasty low-carb foods now in the marketplace ... low-carb breads and other baked goods, low-carb pastas, even low-carb ice cream and candy ... and where to buy them. Roughly 200 new low-carb food products are introduced every month, industry sources report. There's no need to feel deprived on *The Ultimate Low-Carb Plan*.

And we'll give you more Web sites you can visit to gather still more information. Armed with these Internet sources, you will be able to put together a menu plan that's tailored to your personal tastes and needs, one bite at a time. It will let you lose unwanted fat steadily over the coming year and keep it off the rest of your life.

Now, read on, dear reader, and begin winning your own battle of the bulge.

CHAPTER 2

WHAT'S IT ALL ABOUT?

For decades the nutritional establishment has screamed that the only way to lose weight is by cutting back on calories and fat at the same time as you increase physical activity. T'ain't so. In fact, low-fat diets are restrictive and unsatisfying, leaving many dieters feeling deprived, frustrated, sometimes even angry.

Result: They abandon their diets and pig out on their favorite foods, quickly re-gaining the weight they've lost. And they do it over and over again. It's led to what nutritional authorities sometimes call "the yo-yo syndrome" — rapid weight loss on a diet, followed by excessive eating, leading, inevitably, to weight gain. Up and down; up and down. Like a yo-yo.

OK, so what is a low-carb diet and how does it

work? One thing it's NOT is a miracle cure for excess weight. It takes work and thought and effort. To succeed you need to keep careful watch, not only of your carb intake, but of your calories and fats, as well. The best and most successful low-carb diet, we believe, is the one that curtails carb intake, but doesn't ban carbs altogether.

It's true that with a low-carb diet you can indulge in all of the delicious foods denied by low-fat diet plans — seafood in butter, steaks, mayonnaise dressings; eggs, cheese, cream and butter. All those, and more, are allowed. But today, unlike the early days of Atkins, there are low-carb breads, pastas, even ice cream and candy, making it easier to cut carbs AND fats at the same time. In fact, the movement is so huge that food manufacturers, eager to keep up, have been bringing to market around 200 new low-carb products every month.

Our bodies break carbohydrates down into glucose, our main energy source. Simple carbohydrates, found in sugar, processed foods and some fruits, provide an energy boost, but not a lot of nutrients. Complex carbs, found in grains and vegetables, give us energy as well as essential minerals and vitamins. Too many carbs will trigger a sharp increase in your body's production of insulin, which, in turn, will make you more hungry — and cause your body to store nutrients as fat.

The nutritional establishment recommends carbohydrates should make up 55 percent to 60 percent — or more — of total calories in your diet, about 130 grams a day. Americans actually consume about 200 grams a day, authorities report. The result: obesity on a grand scale.

Low-carb diets are based on the body's burning fat as fuel in the absence of carbohydrates. The diets greatly reduce carb consumption so that the body will burn fat quickly. After the dieters achieve their desired weight-loss goal, they gradually add complex carbohydrates back into the diet for balance and maintenance.

Many low-carb diet plans call for as few as 20 grams of carbs a day, at least in the early stages of the diet. Health authorities wring their hands over the potential health hazards of eating too few carbs, though they produce little hard scientific evidence to support the warning.

But isn't it logical to say that if we gain weight on 130 to 200 grams of carbs a day and lose a lot on 20 grams, would we still lose, though perhaps a little less, if we limited our carb intake to, say, 60 grams a day? It makes sense. And we can encourage that weight loss still more if, as we limit our carb intake, we also reduce some of our fat intake.

How can you limit both? Easy. Buy lean meats when you can and when you can't, trim away as much fat as possible. Remove the skin from chicken before you eat it, although many authorities say it's OK to leave the skin on while its cooking. However, if in doubt, remove it. If you're worried about losing juices, wrap the chicken in aluminum foil. And stay far, far away from fried foods — ALL fried foods. Read the labels on every food product you buy. Check for carb counts and fat content. It'll take some thought and some effort and some time, but you CAN do it.

Skip the empty carbs — soft drinks and foods high in sugar and starch. Find alternatives for things like potatoes, rice, beans, breads and pasta. You don't think so? Consider this: A medium cauliflower, boiled then mashed with a little milk and butter, makes a delightful alternative to potatoes. You can even spark it up by putting it into an oven-proof cup with a slice of sharp cheddar on top and putting it under the broiler until the cheese melts and turns brown. That same cauliflower, boiled, can be broken up in your food processor into rice-size particles that taste even better than long grain.

If you drink alcoholic beverages, keep your consumption low, no more than one drink a day for women, two for men. Stay away from wines and sweet liquors; vodka, gin and whiskey have fewer carbs and fewer calories. If you like beer, pick a low-carb product. They are out there now. Avoid soft drinks like the plague.

Learn to read the Nutrition Facts panel on the prepared foods you buy. It'll tell you the number of calories and carbs, as well as a wealth of other useful information, including serving size and number of servings in the package.

But, you may ask, what about breads and baked goods, pastas, candy and other sweet things? Here's a pleasant shocker: There are thousands — yup, *thousands* — of tasty low-carb prepared foods now available, most of them available on the Internet. More about that later.

But you can't lose weight and keep it off with a rigid four-week diet; it takes a change in behavior, a change to a new lifestyle. *The Ultimate Low-Carb Plan* is NOT just a diet — it's the doorway to a new lower weight life.

The right mindset is critically important to a successful diet, say experts at the National Institutes of Health (NIH). Here are a few words of wisdom from the top health agency in America:

● **Setting the right goal is important.** Make your goals short term and very attainable: "I'll walk 30 minutes a day, five days a week," instead of "I'll walk five miles a day"; "I'll cut my carbs and calories by a third this week," rather than "I'll eliminate carbs from my diet." Nothing succeeds like success; achieving a series of small goals will encourage you to continue to larger ones.

● **Be forgiving.** If you don't succeed this week, it's not the end of the world. Just start your diet all over again on Monday. Feeling like a failure goads many people to eat more sweets, fats, carbs — anything that's "comfort food" — to make themselves feel better. It's a trap, so avoid it.

● **When you do achieve a goal, set another.** A successful diet can be built with many small steps, each carrying you a little closer to your ultimate goal.

● **Reward yourself for success** — but NOT with food. Give yourself a mental checkbook and write yourself a reward check for each success. Promise yourself you'll visit the mall, take in a movie, or do anything you don't do very often — but would like to do more — when you achieve a goal.

● **Keep a diary** of what and how often you eat, how often and how much you exercise.

● **Eat more slowly** and chew your food well. How many times have you heard that? But it's true. It takes your brain about 15 minutes to get the message that you're full from your stomach. And you can eat a lot of unneeded food in 15 minutes.

And a few more:

● **Eat only when you're hungry**; don't snack a lot, especially during the evening hours.

● **Eat dinner before 7 p.m.**; going to bed with a full stomach makes it tough for your body to metabolize the food and that opens the door to fat deposits. If your work hours make this impossible, then be sure you eat more than four hours before you go to bed.

● **Watch how much food you put on your plate.** Better two small helpings than one giant helping.

● **Buy an inexpensive portable carb counter** — there are dozens available online — and check out foods before you eat them.

Just four weeks on *The Ultimate Low-Carb Plan* and you'll begin feeling and looking better. Mirrors won't be on your list of things to throw rocks at. And you'll feel better — and feel better about yourself, too. But best of all, when you rid yourself of that excess fat, you'll be healthier and more energetic.

All right; enough advice, already. Now let's take a healthy bite of Dr. Atkins.

CHAPTER 3

A BITE OF DR. ATKINS

The Atkins Diet has been around for 30 years now and at last, thanks to new research, is gaining well-deserved acceptance in the scientific and medical communities.

Although nutritionists still generally hate it because it goes against the basic principle of dieting — THEIR principle — it continues to be an extremely popular weight-loss program and has engendered numerous other similar diet plans.

Conventional nutritional wisdom says that a calorie is a calorie, regardless of where it comes from, and the only way to lose weight is to reduce your caloric intake or dramatically increase your level of physical activity.

Cardiologist Robert Atkins, M.D., maintained that calories alone are not the problem, but rather the *type* of calories we consume is.

He cited carbohydrates as the real culprit in weight gain.

"I believe most overweight people in the world are carbohydrate sensitive," he said. "Cut out carbohydrates and fat automatically becomes the No. 1 fuel."

His diet, then, allows you to eat meat, eggs and fats like butter, but limits your carbs — no potatoes, pasta, rice, breads, sugar or fruit.

Not only do you ignore calories on the Atkins plan, but you eat until you are full, which makes it an easy diet for people to follow.

Dieters can expect to lose a pound a day on the Atkins diet, particularly during the first two weeks, a level of weight loss that brought Dr. Atkins under sharp attack from the nutritional establishment — and brought cheers from the 15 million or so Americans who have bought his books.

The theory behind the Atkins Diet is that by increasing protein and limiting carbs, you trigger a metabolic change that causes the body to use up its stored fat.

"Of the millions of people who have gone on my diet, a large percentage lost weight, kept it off and decisively improved their health," he once said.

Study after study has confirmed that. In one

comparison of the Atkins Diet with the American Heart Association Diet, Dr. Eric Westman at Duke University found that not only did the volunteers in his study lose weight — 31 pounds per person, compared to 20 pounds among those on the Heart Association Diet — but their cholesterol changed for the better, as well.

Since then, a study at Duke has borne out his findings, as has one at the University of Pennsylvania. Nonetheless, die-hard nutritional experts insist the Atkins Diet works only because people reduce the amount they're eating, thereby cutting calories.

Whatever the reason, there is no doubt that many people, especially men, have lost a lot of weight on his diet.

Here are the basic rules:

❑ At the beginning, you can eat no bread, sugar, grains, potatoes, rice, pasta or fruit. But you can eat fish, eggs, pork, beef, lamb, turkey and other meats — as much as you want.

❑ You can have butter and any oil that is liquid at room temperature.

❑ Cheese is limited to 3 to 4 ounces a day.

❑ Three cups of salad vegetables are permitted each day, but other vegetables, including broccoli, zucchini, tomatoes and onions are limited to 1 cup a day.

❑ Avoid sugar in any form, including alcohol,

soda, milk and yogurt; fruit and fruit juice; flour products, cereals, beans, legumes and starchy vegetables like corn, peas and carrots.

❑ You must drink at least 64 ounces of water a day. Herbal teas are OK, but if you drink coffee or regular tea, it must be decaffeinated.

❑ After the first couple of weeks, you can increase your daily carbohydrate intake, adding fruits and other foods. If you follow the plan, Dr. Atkins promised both weight loss and improved general health.

Some experts say many people on the Atkins Diet have trouble resisting their cravings for sweets and starches over the long haul and, thus, "fall off the wagon." And some authorities say a diet that focuses heavily on fat and protein and so little on fiber and carbohydrates can place a too-heavy burden on the liver. Too much protein stresses the liver. Too much fat and too little fiber can affect the heart and digestive system.

An estimated 20 million people have embraced the Atkins Diet — most of them with considerable success.

Dr. Atkins made it clear his plan wasn't merely a short-term diet, but rather a regimen to be followed through life.

The Atkins Diet restricts followers to around 20 grams of carbs a day during the first two weeks. After that, dieters are allowed to increase their carb intake in 5-gram increments until they reach their "maintenance level" — the highest number of carbs they can eat before they begin gaining weight again.

The strict regimen during the first two weeks was designed to take dieters into ketosis, a state in which the body stops producing an over-abundance of insulin and burns off stored fat at a prodigious rate.

In the second phase, dieters are allowed more palatable foods. They can raise the level of veg-etable intake to about 40 grams of carbs a day. During this phase, individuals establish their own personal weight-loss goals. And toward the end of this phase, they determine the highest level of carbs they can consume without re-gain-ing weight. This is the maintenance phase.

Phase 3 of the diet allows more carbs, slowing weight loss. Indeed, under the Atkins philoso-phy, the slower you lose the last five pounds, the better off you will be. In this phase, carb intake is increased until you are losing less than a pound a week.

The final phase is the maintenance diet, which Dr. Atkins said should be followed for life. Here, you may eat as many carbs as you like — as long as you do not begin re-gaining your lost weight.

CHAPTER 4

MYTHS & MISINFORMATION

A short time before his death, I interviewed Dr. Atkins for an article in which he responded to the body of myths his critics have built around his — and, in fact, ALL — low-carb diet plans. He shot them down, one by one, using science as his big gun. These are a few of those myths countered by Dr. Atkins' facts:

MYTH: The Atkins Nutritional Approach is only effective for weight loss because calories are restricted.

FACT: While some of those who do the Atkins Diet may eat fewer calories than before, it is not because the program is restrictive or unduly limits food intake. A high-protein, controlled-carbohydrate diet stabilizes blood sugar throughout the day and that quells the craving for food.

What's more, the Atkins diet calls for foods —
meat, fish, cheese, nuts, eggs, low-sugar,
low-starch vegetables and fruit — that are nutri-
ent-dense and, thus, more satisfying.

Scientific research supports the fact that you
can consume more calories and lose more
weight on a controlled-carbohydrate program
as compared to a low-fat one. For example, in a
12-week study at Schneider Children's Hospital
in New York, one group of obese teenagers was
restricted to 1,100 low-fat calories a day, while a
second group consumed 1,830 calories a day on
a high-protein, controlled-carbohydrate diet.
The second group lost an average of 10.5
pounds more than the low-fat group — and had
lowered total cholesterol and triglyceride levels
and increased HDL (good) cholesterol.

MYTH: The weight lost on the Atkins Nutritional
Approach is mostly water, not fat.

FACT: People do lose some water weight during the first few days of any diet. But research
shows that on a controlled-carbohydrate nutritional approach the water balance soon returns
to normal, and the weight loss comes from fat.
The most dramatic sign of this loss is seeing the
inches drop off your measurements.

MYTH: Ketosis, the backbone of the Atkins
Diet, is dangerous and causes a variety of medical problems.

FACT: Carbohydrates convert to glucose in the body. When you cut back on carbs, you effectively take away most of one of the body's fuels and the body then turns to fat for its energy source and that produces ketones. This is good because the more ketones you produce, the more fat you've burned off. It has no harmful effects but unfortunately, ketosis sometimes is confused with ketoacidosis, a condition found in diabetics whose blood sugar is out of control, in alcoholics and in individuals who are starving.

The most important point is that ketones really are the fuel that fat delivers when it is used as fuel. The whole purpose of a low-carbohydrate diet is to make fat the primary energy source or fuel — when you cut out carbohydrates, fat is the only choice the body has to get energy. When that happens,0000 the fat turns into ketones and the ketones provide the energy. To say this is dangerous is the same as saying burning up your body fat is dangerous.

MYTH: Diets that promote a liberal intake of high-fat meats and dairy products raise cholesterol levels, ultimately leading to heart disease.

FACT: Study after study has proved that low-carb diets lower cholesterol. There are two sources of energy to fuel our bodies: glucose and fat. When you sufficiently restrict carbohydrates, you will force your body to predominantly burn fat for energy. When you burn dietary fat for energy, it is metabolized rather than stored and therefore poses no serious health risks. Your stored body fat is also burned. That's why not long after you start doing Atkins, a blood test will reveal a lower level of triglycerides, which will bring down your total cholesterol and raise your good (HDL) cholesterol.

MYTH: Because it excludes fruits, vegetables and grains, Atkins is deficient in nutrients.

FACT: The Atkins Nutritional Approach does not exclude fruits, vegetables and grains. In the opening days of the plan, people are told to consume no more than 20 grams of carbohydrates a day — these in leafy salads or high-fiber vegetables such as broccoli, asparagus, eggplant or spinach. Later, they may increase that to as much as 60 to 90 grams. "You keep adding vegetables until you stop losing weight," Dr. Atkins explains. "Then you know what your carbohydrate level for losing is and you have to spend the rest of your weight-loss phase in the diet under that level or you won't lose any more weight. I've been on the diet since 1963 and I'd bet I eat more vegetables than the average vegetarian."

In the opening days of the diet, people are allowed an amazing 2,000 calories a day, he says — but NOT things like sugar, white flour, milk, white rice, bread, pasta, cookies, ice cream and junk foods.

The start-up phase of the Atkins plan, the most restrictive, was run through a computer analysis used to train nutritionists at universities, he says. The result: the diet exceeded the Recommended Daily Allowance (RDA) of almost all nutrients.

MYTH: The Atkins Nutritional Approach causes constipation because it lacks fiber.

FACT: The Atkins Nutritional Approach includes fiber-rich foods such as spinach, eggplant, broccoli, asparagus and leafy greens. After the start-up phase, it also includes low-sugar fruits such as berries. If more fiber is needed, a fiber supplement such as wheat bran or flax meal is recommended. Supplementation is unnecessary in the Ongoing Weight-Loss phase and beyond because more fruits and vegetables are introduced.

MYTH: People following the Atkins Nutritional Approach may suffer from fatigue.

FACT: Fatigue may occur in the first few days of doing Atkins, while the body adapts to switching metabolic pathways. It typically takes about three to four days for the body to switch from sugar metabolism to fat metabolism. After the transition, as long as individuals do not skip meals, they are able to maintain high energy and clear thinking throughout the day because blood sugar is stabilized.

MYTH: The Atkins Nutritional Approach is deficient in bone-building calcium.

FACT: Atkins offers a variety of foods rich in calcium, including cheese and vegetables such as broccoli and spinach. In one study published in the *American Journal of Nutrition*, researchers reported men on high-meat diets, such as Atkins, had no significant changes in calcium levels.

MYTH: Atkins is high in fat and fats cause gallbladder disease.

FACT: There is now overwhelming scientific evidence that gallstones are formed when fat intake is low because the gallbladder will not contract unless fat is taken in, and if it doesn't contract, stones form. Gallbladders need to be kept active to prevent stone formation.

All right. Now for a big bite of The Zone.

CHAPTER 5

IN THE ZONE – DIET OF THE STARS

You can shed as much as 17 to 20 pounds of unwanted weight in just eight weeks — and get remarkable health benefits, as well — by getting into The Zone, a fabulous low-carb diet plan created by Barry Sears, Ph.D., a former research scientist at M.I.T. And you can do it without feeling hungry, deprived or frustrated, Sears promises.

The Zone concept, now described in several best-selling books, was conceived by Sears after he learned he is genetically programmed for a heart attack in his 50s — his father, uncles and grandfather all died of heart disease in midlife.

"For years, food gurus have told Americans they can slim down by avoiding fats and eating plenty of carbohydrates, like pastas, bread and rice," Sears said. "The result: People follow that advice — and get fat anyway.

"The growing epidemic of obesity in America is not caused by excess fat consumption (which has actually decreased by 14 percent during the past 15 years), but by increased carbohydrate consumption.

"It is impossible for dietary fat alone to make you fat. It is excessive levels of the hormone insulin that makes you fat and keeps you fat. How do you increase insulin levels? By eating too many fat-free carbohydrates or too many calories at any one meal. Americans do both.

"Fat slows the entry of carbohydrates into the bloodstream, thereby decreasing the production of insulin. Since it's insulin that makes you fat, having more fat in the diet is important for reducing insulin, especially since it does not stimulate insulin production. The best type of fat is monounsaturated fat, like olive oil, avocado, almonds and macadamia nuts," noted Sears.

"You can use food as a hormonal ATM card. The average American male or female carries a minimum of 100,000 calories of stored body fat. To put this in perspective, this amount of stored body fat is equivalent to eating 1,700 pancakes. That's a pretty big breakfast. The calories you need for energy are already stored in your body. What you need is a hormonal ATM card to release them.

"Carbohydrates are a drug. The body needs a certain amount of carbohydrates at every meal for optimal brain function, just like a drug. However, excessive consumption of any drug leads to toxic side effects. The side effect of an overdose of carbohydrates at any meal is excess production of insulin and that can be dangerous to your health," Sears explained.

"The only drug that can control that insulin production is food. By eating an appropriate amount of protein, carbohydrates and fats at each meal or snack, you can keep your insulin in balance. That balance is 'The Zone'.

"Almost magically, metabolic changes occur in The Zone. Excess fat cells are used as fuel by the body, giving you more energy as you lose weight.

"You will lose about 1.5 pounds of pure fat every week you're in The Zone and during the first two weeks, you'll also shed about five pounds of water that is stored in your body as you lower your insulin levels. By the end of eight weeks, the average person can lose 17 to 20 pounds in total weight — without ever feeling deprived, frustrated or half-starved.

"And perhaps best of all, recent scientific studies have demonstrated that being in The Zone can decrease your risk of heart disease and diabetes, give you better protection against arthritis and osteoporosis, and beef up your body's natural defenses against infection and disease — and there is even evidence suggesting it may lower a woman's risk of breast cancer.

"So The Zone Diet is not just a plan for eating better — it's a prescription for a lifetime of better health," concluded Sears.

And it's become a way of life in Hollywood, where a trim figure and youthful appearance add up to money in the bank. And the stars gush glowingly about their "wonderful diet."

Here's what just a few of them have had to say:

• Country singing legend Dolly Parton said she was "delighted" to drop 20 pounds: "I'll spread the meals from early morning to evening. But they aren't huge fattening meals. They're small, healthy, low-calorie and it's enough food to make me satisfied. The Zone's a lot more sensible than fasting or eating nothing but watermelon. I love this kind of diet!"

• Sandra Bullock, a self-confessed one-time junk-food junkie: "I've lost 13 pounds and I've taken three-and-a-half inches off my butt." Bullock was an early subscriber to Annie's Edibles, celebrity chef Annalisa Mastroianni's catering service to the stars — at $400 a week for three meals and two snacks a day. Mastroianni says most of her meals are prepared according to Zone principles — with variations according to individual stars' personal preferences. Bullock, for example, won't eat raw onions or garlic and Matthew McConaughey, another Zonehead, favors shrimp VeraCruz, Mastroianni reports.

• David James Elliott, star of the popular series *JAG*: "It's a challenge, staying in shape on a series. We're working 12- to 14-hour days, so there's never enough time for a real workout and you've got to watch what you eat because by hour 14 you're so tired you just start slamming sugar. (The Zone) was great because it gave me a road map to eating."

• Supermodel Lisa Ray: "I'm the opposite of a health nut, I love food and I eat like a sow, but now I'm an enthusiastic convert to Dr. Barry Sears' concept of eating in 'The Zone' This largely involves reducing simple carbohydrates in your diet to lose weight and regain energy. I used to laugh at other people talking about things like this, but my energy levels are just soaring — I sound just like one of those fanatics. Finding out about The Zone has been one of the most exciting things in my life!"

In fact, The Zone Diet is so hot in Hollywood that celebrity Zoneheads congregate most days at the famed Los Angeles Farm in Santa Monica, a favorite dining place for the stars (Barbra Streisand dines there often), where The Zone is on the lunch menu all of the time.

Take a bite of some of these simple rules, straight out of The Zone:

● Always eat within an hour of waking.

● Eat at least three meals and two snacks every day. Afternoon and late evening snacks are critically important. "A Zone meal should give you 4 to 5 hours in The Zone, a Zone snack 2 to 2.5 hours," Sears explains. "You must eat every 4 to 5 hours after a meal or 2 to 2.5 hours after a snack, hungry or not, to stay in The Zone."

● Lack of hunger and clear mental focus are excellent barometers that you are in The Zone. Before every meal and snack always assess your hunger and mental focus.

● Every meal and snack starts with low-fat protein plus carbohydrates (eat more leafy green vegetables and fruits and less starch-like carbohydrates, such as pasta, breads, rice and grains) and don't forget "good" fats like olive oil.

● A typical serving of low-fat protein should fit in and be no thicker than the palm of your hand. A typical snack contains one ounce of protein for both men and women. At first, a kitchen scale is helpful to measure the protein portion. You can soon eyeball these amounts at home, in restaurants and fast-food take-outs.

"If you follow the eye-and-palm method, you'll wind up with roughly 40 percent of the calories on your plate in carbohydrates, 30 percent in protein and 30 percent in fat — a perfect balance," says Sears.

"You'll be getting adequate amounts of protein and fat, and replacing much of the
high-density carbohydrates (grains, pasta, rice,
bread) with lower-density carbohydrates (fruits
and vegetables)."

● Divide your plate into three equal sections.
Put the protein on one-third, fruits and vegetables on the other two-thirds. Don't forget a dash
of fat, such as olive oil.

"Remember, if you make a mistake, your next
Zone meal or snack will take you right back to
The Zone," says Sears. "And even if you're only in
The Zone 70 or 80 percent of the time, you'll
still get 70 or 80 percent of the benefits. You will
soon learn that the longer you're in The Zone,
the less you will crave carbohydrates. In fact, I
suggest a monthly 'pig-out' meal when you eat as
much pasta, rice and bread as you want, just to
feel miserable the next day. This will reinforce
how powerful food can be as a drug."

CHAPTER 6

FLUSH YOUR FAT AWAY

You can even erase your cellulite the way celebrities do, with an off-the-shelf product you can buy at most well-stocked supermarkets — unsweetened cranberry juice, a top nutritional expert reveals.

"It's the best-kept secret in Hollywood," said nationally acclaimed nutritional authority Ann Louise Gittleman, Ph.D., C.N.S., author of the best-selling book *The Fat Flush Plan*, a nutritional program that counts cranberry juice as a key element.

"I get a lot of calls now from agents and assistants just before big Hollywood events," says Gittleman. "The stars want me to talk them through the program, even though they could just read the book and get the same information.

Then I'll see them on the award shows and premieres looking great! I can't give you their names, but this is the program many celebrities turn to when that awards show gown has to fit!"

What's it all about?

It's all about flushing toxins and fats out of the liver, helping it to function more efficiently, explains Gittleman, former nutrition director of the Pritikin Longevity Center. That's why she calls it The Fat Flush Plan.

It's divided into three phases:

1. The two-week Fat Flush — a "boot camp" period designed to flush the liver and get it back to maximum function, at the same time you lose weight.

2. The on-going Fat Flush — Continuation of weight loss, but with a bit more variety in foods and allowing for addition of one "friendly" carb each week.

3. The eating plan for life — The maintenance program, to be followed for life.

It's very restrictive, prohibiting margarine, alcohol, sugar, oils or fats except flaxseed oil; starchy vegetables such as beans, potatoes, corn, parsnips, carrots, peas, pumpkin, acorn or butternut squash, grains, bread, cereal and all dairy products.

Scientists say the liver is the body's work horse, performing more than 400 different functions, some of them critical to maintaining a healthy weight, observes Gittleman.

It breaks down fat and filters out impurities that cause fluid retention and cellulite formation. But Americans today put so many impurities into their bodies — everything from car exhaust fumes to chemical food additives — that the liver can become clogged or even damaged, she says.

And most people don't get enough of those nutrients that help the liver function. That makes matters worse. A poorly functioning liver contributes to overall body fat — and to cellulite — because the unfiltered toxins get into the blood stream, promoting formation of cellulite.

Essentially, the Fat Flush Plan is designed to push unneeded fat and toxins out of the body by maximizing the function of the liver.

A mixture of unsweetened cranberry juice and ground flax seed is a key component, and she calls it "the long-life cocktail."

The long-life cocktail is a combination of the unsweetened cranberry juice and water — an ounce of juice to seven ounces water — and twice a day add one tablespoon of ground flax seeds or one teaspoon of psyllium, she says. For best results, drink two quarts of the cocktail every day for two weeks.

Cranberry juice is chock full of elements that

help in the digestion of fat. The ruby-red berries also contain helpful substances that aren't found in any other food.

If you can't easily find unsweetened cranberry juice, try buying fresh cranberries and making your own. Add one pound of berries to five cups of water and bring it to a boil. When the berries pop, strain the mixture. What you have left will be pure, unsweetened cranberry juice.

Put ground flax seed in the unsweetened cranberry juice and water and you've got something that will balance your hormones, help you with elimination and regularity, make your skin look beautiful and detoxify your liver, says Gittleman.

This cocktail targets the health of the liver. It helps to remove toxins from the system, opens up the liver's two detox pathways and provides adequate fiber to block absorption of bad fats, increase their excretion and bind toxins so they are not reabsorbed into the body.

"Cranberry juice is one of my secret weapons against cellulite because I have observed its ability to emulsify the fatty globules in the lymphatic system, that garbage collector of the body which transports all kinds of waste products and fats not processed by the liver from the blood to the cells," says Gittleman.

Unsweetened cranberry juice is a potent source of phytonutrients and antioxidants, she adds, and these help strengthen connective tissue — the weakening of which is one of the causes of cellulite.

Unsweetened cranberry juice can be found in most health-food stores and well-stocked supermarkets.

But while cranberry juice is a driving force behind the Fat Flush Plan, there are other nutrients that can speed your body's disposal of cellulite — and all unwanted fat, she says.

Without harsh stimulants like ephedra or caffeine, the Fat Flush Plan contains other key elements, which trigger both fat and weight loss safely and simply. Some of these include:

● **A daily dose of fat burning GLA** (gamma linolenic acid) in the form of black currant seed oil helps to trigger fat burning instead of fat storage, contributing still more to control of cellulite. Plus, it reportedly assists in the control of PMS symptoms and wards off skin problems, rheumatoid arthritis and diabetic neuropathy. The pills come in different strengths. The GLA content of each pill is marked on the bottle. You should take as many pills as needed to give you a total of 360 mg a day.

● **Daily CLA** (conjugated linolenic acid) for the lifestyle (third) phase of the Fat Flush Plan. In a 90-day double-blind trial in Norway, participants showed a stunning 20 percent decrease in body fat. CLA has recently been found to protect the body from depositing regained weight as fat to an impressive degree. And it reportedly helps to burn fat, retain lean muscle mass and acts as a powerful antioxidant in the system.

CLA is found in grass-fed beef and the dairy products from grass-fed animals. But since much of our livestock is no longer grass-fed, you need to take supplements. Take one pill, containing one gram of CLA, with each meal.

● **Flax seed oil** is another major contributor to the benefits from the Fat Flush Plan. Each tablespoon provides enough omega-3 fatty acids — which regulate insulin, the hormone that controls the body's storage of fat — to pick up the slack from a poorly functioning liver at the same time they bind to oil-soluble poisons that help create cellulite and carry them out of the body. Flax seed oil is sold as a liquid and can be found in many supermarkets. Take two tablespoons a day and use only in dishes that are not heated or cooked.

Flax seed oil provides the satiety factor that also revs up the metabolism, stops hunger and puts an end to the fatigue and deprivation that can make you tempted to cheat on your diet. Plus, flax seeds themselves can be used as a fiber source to bind up fat and transport it out of the system. As a source of plant sterols, flax seeds boost immune function.

The Fat Flush Plan features a number of other unusual foods not found in other weight-loss regimens. Like eggs and meat, for example. Now found in most supermarkets, omega-3 enriched eggs — especially the yolks — are included in the menus for every phase of the plan because they provide the highest concentration of sulfur-bearing amino acids and essential fatty acids so vital to the liver's ability to burn fats effectively.

They contribute greatly to the liver's production of bile. And bile breaks down fat. So it was no surprise when another study showed dieters who ate two eggs a day for six weeks had significant weight loss, especially around the waistline.

Also, omega-3s have been shown to speed metabolism and reduce hunger by as much as 20 percent.

Beef is on the Fat Flush Plan menu because it is the highest dietary source of an incredibly effective nutrient that transports fat into muscle cells so it can be burned, especially when the body is already in a fat-burning mode. If you can find grass-fed beef, eat four ounces at least twice a week.

And you can have up to eight ounces of protein a day — seafood, chicken, lamb or grass-fed beef — which will raise your metabolism by 25 percent. And the higher your metabolism, the more fat you burn off.

You can help the fat flush process along by eating a lot of vegetables, which release "fat magnets" into your body, Gittleman says. These fibrous magnets attach themselves to fat globules and toxins and carry them out of your system before they can be absorbed. You can eat as many vegetables as you want — broccoli, asparagus, cucumbers, tomatoes, spaghetti squash, green leafy vegetables, sprouts and more.

You also can have up to two portions of fresh fruit a day, which will provide the body with enzymes that help with digestions and repair body tissues.

"Vegetables also are chock full of natural enzymes, vitamins and minerals, particularly potassium, which reduces fluid retention in the body that can be caused by a poorly functioning liver, Gittleman says.

"Although many of us are adopting a lower carb, higher protein and higher fat eating plan, most Americans are still missing the boat when it comes to long-term health and quality nutrition. For starters, cutting out all carbs, including those antioxidant-rich, colorful vegetables and fruits, means losing out on rejuvenating chlorophyll, enzymes, vitamins, minerals and cleansing fiber. And this is just one of the reasons why Fat Flush is the healthiest and most effective low-carb diet option of them all!"

according to its creator. "You can drop at least two dress or pant sizes right from the start with the Two Week Fat Flush phase, at the same time you lower cholesterol levels, balance blood sugar, relieve depression, improve sleep, achieve higher energy levels and optimize breast and prostate protection from cancer.

"And there are both men and women who have lost up to 125 pounds without a trace of the hanging skin or 'hang dog' look that comes with some weight-loss programs.

"Your liver is strongly affected by a poor diet. Excess fat, sugar, alcohol and caffeine — even diet soda, antidepressants and birth control pills — help to create a tired and toxic liver that can't efficiently burn body fat and thus can sabotage your weight-loss efforts.

"The Fat Flush Plan is designed to clean out the liver and help you drop a dress size or two and get rid of that ugly cellulite.

"Probably nothing you do to control your weight is as important as keeping your liver healthy.

"There is room for plenty of variety in the Fat Flush Plan, no boringly severe restrictions. And those who've used the plan, we call them Flushers, say they have found it also improves circulation, increases energy, helps with sleep, stabilizes mood swings, helps the skin and nails look better and lowers anxiety and depression.

Moreover, the plan can lower cholesterol by as much as 30 points," Gittleman continues.

"Fat Flush is dedicated to promoting a balanced lifestyle for long-term health and it champions simple healthy habits we all tend to overlook or forget about as a result of life in these hectic days. The use of the right kinds of fats, culinary herbs and spices, lean proteins and phytonutrient-dense veggies and fruits can speed up weight loss, remove bloat and provide profound detoxifying benefits for your entire body."

Now let's take a healthy stroll down South Beach.

CHAPTER 7

THE SOUTH BEACH DIET

This hot, new diet hails from Miami's body-obsessed South Beach, where sexy celebrities like Ricky Martin and Gloria Estefan are known to strut their stuff. It was created by University of Miami cardiologist Arthur Agatston, M.D., whose book, *The South Beach Diet*, is a screaming best seller.

The common-sense plan was originally developed as a cholesterol-lowering program for patients with high levels of "bad" cholesterol and triglycerides and for pre-diabetics with high blood glucose levels. But when Dr. Agatston observed patients were losing up to 14 pounds during the first two weeks and two pounds a week after that, he enlarged the plan in *The South Beach Diet*, a book that hit the top of the best-seller lists last year with more than 7 million copies sold.

Unlike the Atkins plan, which promotes consumption of fatty meats like hamburgers and bacon, and The Zone Diet, which makes you break meals into "blocks" based on certain percentages, the South Beach Diet urges you to eat healthy fats found in olive oil and fish, which are rich in omega-3 fatty acids, and to enjoy the foods you are used to, so you won't feel deprived.

Since his book was published, Dr. Agatston has made a few changes. In the book, for example, eggs were one of the approved foods, but today his recipes call for egg substitutes.

To avoid feeling hungry, South Beach recommends eating normal-size portions at each meal, plus snacks in mid-morning and afternoon. The catch: You must restrict your intake of certain foods during the first two weeks. Here's the breakdown:

● Spreading your intake of good carbs and good fats over three meals and two snacks will help balance your blood glucose, insulin and cholesterol. And that balance will reduce feelings of hunger and, some say, cravings for sweets and other carbs.

● South Beach is high in proteins and fiber, low in carbs and animal fats. And it does not require you to count carbs, calories or fats.

The bottom line, though: During the first two phases of South Beach, you will be able to eat between 1,200 and 1,600 calories a day and in the third phase you can kick that up to 1,600 to 2,000. No one is going to go hungry on South Beach.

During the two-week Phase One of South Beach, you can eat meat, chicken, turkey, fish and shellfish. And you may have salads and drink coffee or tea. But starches, like bread, potatoes, rice, pasta and baked goods, as well as all fruit, are on the "No-No" list. So are beer, wine and other alcoholic drinks.

People who get past that First Phase say afterward that they lose their craving for sweets and starches very quickly. And when Phase One is over, you can begin adding the banished foods and beverages back into your diet. The trick is in picking which foods to add, because they are not all allowed at the same time — which can make the diet a bit difficult for some.

Phase Two of South Beach continues until your reach your ultimate weight goal, however long that takes. Typically, people lose a pound or two a week. And Phase Three is the diet-for-life plan, allowing you to eat pretty much as much as you want.

Here are typical one-day menu plans for each phase of the diet:

PHASE ONE

Phase One might be tough for those who really crave pasta, bread and sugary substances, including fruit. But the good news is that it only last two weeks — and you can have six mini-meals a day.

BREAKFAST: Six oz. of V-8 juice, a two-egg omelette with one tablespoon of shredded cheddar cheese; decaf coffee or tea with fat-free milk and a sugar substitute.

MID-MORNING SNACK: Two slices of rolled turkey breast.

LUNCH: Shrimp Caesar Salad (no croutons) with two tablespoons of Caesar dressing.

MID-AFTERNOON SNACK: Two slices of feta cheese over 1/2 of a sliced tomato and six slices of cucumber.

DINNER: Grilled salmon and steamed spinach.

DESSERT: One sugar-free popsicle.

PHASE TWO

During Phase Two, you'll slowly introduce some high-fiber carbs back into your diet. These might include sweet potatoes, whole-grain rice and pasta, some fruits, cereal and a slice of bread.

BREAKFAST: One cup low-fat yogurt topped with fresh blueberries; decaf coffee or tea with fat-free milk and a sugar substitute.

MID-MORNING SNACK: One hard-boiled egg.

LUNCH: Chef's salad with one oz. each of mozzarella cheese and chicken over lettuce, one sliced tomato and two tablespoons of vinaigrette dressing.

MID-AFTERNOON SNACK: 1/2 grapefruit.

DINNER: 6 oz. of grilled chicken breast; six steamed asparagus spears, 1/2 steamed sweet potato.

DESSERT: 4 oz. fat-free, sugar-free pudding.

PHASE THREE

This is the maintenance phase of South Beach. It allows the most liberal choices of foods, so you can learn which ones make you re-gain weight and which will let you stay at your ideal weight. You're allowed snacks during this phase, but most people don't feel the need. If you begin to re-gain, simply go back to Phase Two for a week or two.

BREAKFAST: 1 cup of strawberries; 1/2 toasted bagel with cottage cheese; decaf coffee or tea with fat-free milk and a sugar substitute.

LUNCH: 4 oz. of grilled lean hamburger patty on 1/2 of a whole-wheat bun; coleslaw, pickles, sliced tomato and lettuce.

DINNER: 2 pork chops; mushrooms sauteed in olive oil; steamed brussels sprouts with lemon.

DESSERT: One cup of plain, nonfat yogurt topped with chopped peaches or apricots.

CHAPTER 8

YOUR ULTIMATE LOW-CARB PLAN

*T*he *Ultimate Low-Carb Plan* has five distinct parts, each of them easy to learn, easy to follow — designed to help you slough off as much as 20 pounds of unwanted fat over the first 8 weeks.

STAGE ONE

Take a bunch of tiny bites. Take one from Atkins, another from The Zone. Nibble a while on the Fat Flush Plan, then kick up a little sand from South Beach. Read each of these great diet programs and pick the elements that you'd be comfortable with. Yes, I know; that's four books — a lot of reading and some expense. But they're "keepers," worth reading, worth buying. And if you don't feel you can afford them, try your public library.

STAGE TWO

Count some Cs. Carbs and calories, that is. Read the chapter on menu plans, study the sample five-day plans for women and men, then pick the low-carb recipes that sound appealing and build your own 30-day menu.

One of the major problems with all diets is that people start them, lose a few pounds, back-slide and gain back not only those pounds, but more. There's that yo-yo syndrome again. Why does it happen? Surely we WANT to lose weight? We WANT to look better, feel better, be more healthy.

Think about it. Every diet, ANY diet, is a radical change from your normal, customary eating habits. And anything that's radical is hard to follow.

So forget limiting yourself to an unsatisfying 20 to 30 carbs a day; start out at 100 for the first four weeks. Uncle Sam's nutritional experts recommend we eat 130 grams of carbohydrates a day and report most Americans gobble down 200. By cutting back to 100, your are radically reducing your carb intake. It may be a little difficult at first, but you CAN do it.

Each week, include more whole fresh fruits and vegetables into your diet, and cut back still more on starches and processed foods. And after four weeks, it'll be as easy as a low-carb pie.

That's when we start getting tough. At the

four-week mark, cut your carbs back to 60 to 70 a day. Now we're getting down to some potentially serious weight loss, especially if you've been cutting back on fats, as you should, at the same time.

Initially, you'll lose a lot of water weight; that happens with every diet. But then your body will begin burning stored fats and that's when you'll start taking off pounds and returning to that 20-something waistline.

You can speed up the process by slowing your consumption of soft drinks during the first four weeks, then cutting them out entirely, along with anything containing corn syrup.

STAGE THREE

Get Moving. Add enough daily activities to your life to burn off 7,000 calories a week. Sound like a lot? Read the chapter on exercise and you'll see it's not a lot at all. And it'll melt away as much as two pounds of flab each week.

STAGE FOUR

Cancel your snack attacks. In the chapter on snacking you'll learn how. Bottom line: Americans are the world's champion snackers, especially in the evening. I won't ask you to stop entirely; just cut back a little and use some of the great low-carb snacks now in the marketplace — cookies, candies, ice cream and more. Yummm!

STAGE FIVE

Take a leap into cyberspace. Sound scary? It's not. If you're new to the Internet, here's the perfect guide: your 9-year-old. Or if you don't have one, a friend's or a neighbor's child. The Internet is as familiar to most kids today as their backyards.

There are three chapters dealing with cyberspace.

The first will give you the addresses of some wonderful Internet sites where you can gather a wealth of information, guidance and support while you shed your unwanted pounds. And you'll find new information, based on the most cutting-edge scientific research, being added almost daily.

The second will give you a carb counter prepared by experts at the Food and Nutrition Service of the U.S. Department of Agriculture and will guide you to the department's Internet site where you will find a search engine that will let you learn all the nutritional values of every conceivable food. I'll tell you how to use it.

And the third will show you a list of just some of the thousands of low-carb and diet aids now available on the Internet, with addresses of some online stores and instructions on how to find many, many more.

That's it; that's *The Ultimate Low-Carb Plan.*

A "miracle diet"? Nope; just some old-fashioned common sense. Tough to follow? Not at all; a little effort and a little thought and you'll almost be able to watch your fat flying out the window.

So, let's get to it. See you when you're thin, maybe along South Beach with the stars.

CHAPTER 9

LET'S EAT

You can put together a great 30-day menu plan by watching the carbs you eat, making sure to keep the daily load to a maximum of 60 to 70 grams at the same time you cut back where possible on fats.

To make that easier, on the following pages are two five-day sample low-carb menu plans, one for women, one for men, prepared by Barry Sears, Ph.D., author of *The Zone*.

JUST FOR WOMEN

DAY 1

BREAKFAST:
3 oz. Canadian bacon

Fruit salad of 2/3 cup mandarin oranges and
3/4 cup blueberries sprinkled with
3 tsp. slivered almonds

LUNCH:
1 large tossed salad containing:
1 cup lettuce
1/4 cup chickpeas
1 cup chopped mushrooms
2/3 cup sliced celery
1 Tablespoon olive oil & vinegar dressing
3 oz. deli-style turkey breast
1 oz. reduced-fat cheese
1 pear

AFTERNOON SNACK (Make up your own snacks from the ingredients listed on pages 76-77.)

DINNER:
4 1/2 oz. fish fillet of your choice
1 teaspoon olive oil
lemon or ginger slices
2 tomatoes, split, sprinkled with Parmesan
cheese and broiled
1 cup cooked green beans
1/2 cup grapes
*Brush fish with 1 tsp. olive oil. Place lemon or
ginger slices on top. Broil 10 minutes per inch of
thickness. Do not turn.*

EVENING SNACK

DAY 2

BREAKFAST:
   1 cup plain, low-fat yogurt mixed with:
      1/2 cup cubed pineapple
      3 teaspoons slivered almonds
   1 oz. Canadian bacon or 3 turkey bacon strips
served on the side

LUNCH:
   1 mini pita pocket, cut in half, pizza style
   1 oz. reduced-fat cheese
   2 oz. lean chicken breast
   green pepper and onion, chopped, enough to
top pizza

AFTERNOON SNACK

DINNER:
   3 oz. chicken breast cut into strips
   1 teaspoon olive oil
   1 cup chopped onion
   1 1/2 cups broccoli florets
   1 1/2 cups sliced mushrooms
   1 plum
   Sauté chicken in a nonstick pan. Add onions,

broccoli and mushrooms. Stir-fry on medium heat.

EVENING SNACK

"By the end of Day 2, you should be thinking significantly more clearly because you won't be getting the afternoon drops in attention caused by eating too many carbohydrates," Sears says.

DAY 3

BREAKFAST:
4 egg whites or 1/2 cup egg substitute
sprinkling of low-fat mozzarella cheese
1 teaspoon olive oil
1 cup grapes
2/3 cup cubed honeydew melon
Spray a nonstick pan with vegetable spray. Beat egg white with olive oil and a little milk if desired. Fold in cheese. Scramble.

LUNCH:
3 oz. tuna mixed with:
   1 tablespoon olive oil & vinegar dressing
   chopped celery
1 side salad
1/2 a cantaloupe stuffed with 1/2 cup boysen-berries

AFTERNOON SNACK

DINNER:
  4 1/2 oz. fish fillet of your choice (flounder is recommended)
  sprinkling of Parmesan cheese
  freshly ground pepper, to taste
  squirt of lemon juice
  chopped onion, to taste
  1 side salad
  1 tablespoon olive oil & vinegar dressing
  2 cups cooked green beans
  1/2 apple
  Preheat oven to 425° F. Tear off a large piece of foil. Spray the center lightly with vegetable spray. Put fish in the center of the foil. Top with onion, pepper, lemon juice and cheese. Fold foil over fish, leaving space around the fish. Carefully turn up and seal the ends and the middle so that juices don't leak out. Bake for 18 minutes. Open foil carefully to prevent steam burns.

EVENING SNACK

"By the end of Day 3, you should feel significantly increased energy levels, both mentally and physically," says Sears.

DAY 4

BREAKFAST:
   3/4 cup low-fat cottage cheese
   1 cup pineapple
   1/3 cup mandarin oranges
   3 macadamia nuts
   Mix together and enjoy.

LUNCH:
   1 soy burger patty
   1 oz. reduced-fat cheese
   lettuce and tomato slice
   dill pickle wedge (optional)
   1 teaspoon reduced-fat mayonnaise
   1 side salad
   2 teaspoons olive oil & vinegar dressing
   1 cup unsweetened applesauce, sprinkled with cinnamon
   Spray nonstick pan with vegetable spray. Cook soy burger according to package directions.

AFTERNOON SNACK

DINNER:
   3 oz. chicken breast, no skin
   lemon slices
   onion slices
   1 to 2 teaspoons barbecue sauce

1 cup green beans sauteed in garlic with
3 teaspoons slivered almonds
1 apple
*Preheat oven to 450° F. Cover chicken breast
with slices of onion and lemon. Bake for 15 minutes. Reduce heat to 350°. Baste with barbecue
sauce. Cook for 10 to 15 minutes or until done.*

EVENING SNACK

By Day 4, your carbohydrate cravings — the
desire for a cookie, or other sweets in the afternoon — will have dropped dramatically.

DAY 5

BREAKFAST:

6 egg white omelet with 1/2 cup of vegetables
sauteed with 2 teaspoons of olive oil
2/3 cup of slow-cooked oatmeal
1 cup strawberries

LUNCH:

Grilled chicken Caesar Salad with (3 oz. of
chicken)
2 cups grilled vegetables
1 apple

AFTERNOON SNACK

DINNER:
    5 oz. grilled salmon
    1 small garden salad
    4 cups steamed vegetables
    1 cup mixed berries

EVENING SNACK

JUST FOR MEN

DAY 1

BREAKFAST:
    4 oz. Canadian bacon
    Fruit salad of:
    2/3 cup mandarin oranges
    1 cup strawberries
    3/4 cup blueberries sprinkled with 4
teaspoons slivered almonds

LUNCH:
    1 large tossed salad containing:
      1 cup lettuce
      1/2 cup chickpeas
      1 cup chopped mushrooms
      2/3 cup sliced celery
      2 Tablespoons olive oil & vinegar dressing

    3 oz. deli-style turkey breast
    2 oz. reduced-fat cheese
  1 pear

AFTERNOON SNACK (Make up your own snacks from the ingredients listed on pages 76-77.)

DINNER:
    6 oz. fish fillet of your choice
    1 teaspoon olive oil
    lemon or ginger slices
    2 tomatoes, split, sprinkled with Parmesan cheese & broiled
    1 cup cooked green beans
    1 cup grapes
  Brush fish with olive oil. Place lemon slices on top. Broil 10 minutes per inch of thickness. Do not turn.

EVENING SNACK

DAY 2

BREAKFAST:
    1 1/2 cups plain, low-fat yogurt mixed with:
      1 cup cubed pineapple
      3 teaspoons slivered almonds
    1 oz. Canadian bacon or 3 turkey bacon strips (served on the side)

LUNCH:

1 mini pita pocket, cut in half pizza style

2 oz. reduced-fat cheese

2 oz. lean chicken breast

green pepper and onion, chopped, enough to top pizza

1/2 apple

AFTERNOON SNACK

DINNER:

4 oz. chicken breast cut into strips

1 1/3 teaspoons olive oil

1 cup chopped onion

1 1/2 cups broccoli florets

1 1/2 cups sliced mushrooms

1 orange

Sauté chicken in a nonstick pan. Add onions, broccoli and mushrooms. Stir-fry on medium heat.

EVENING SNACK

DAY 3

BREAKFAST:

6 egg whites or 3/4 cup egg substitute

sprinkling of low-fat mozzarella cheese

1 1/3 teaspoons olive oil

1 cup grapes
1/2 cup blueberries
2/3 cup cubed honeydew melon
Spray a nonstick pan with vegetable spray. Beat egg white with olive oil and a little milk if desired. Fold in cheese. Scramble.

LUNCH:

4 oz. tuna mixed with:
    4 teaspoons olive oil & vinegar dressing
    chopped celery
1 side salad
1/2 cantaloupe stuffed with:
    1/2 cup boysenberries and
    1 cup raspberries

AFTERNOON SNACK

DINNER:

6 oz. fish fillet of your choice (flounder is recommended)
sprinkling of Parmesan cheese
freshly ground pepper, to taste
squirt of lemon juice
chopped onion, to taste
1 side salad
4 teaspoons olive oil & vinegar dressing
2 cups cooked green beans
1 apple

Preheat oven to 425° F. Tear off a large piece of foil. Spray the center lightly with vegetable spray. Put fish in the center of the foil. Top with onion, pepper, lemon juice and cheese. Fold foil over fish, leaving space around the fish. Carefully turn up and seal the ends and the middle so that juices don't leak out. Bake for 18 minutes. Open foil carefully to prevent steam burns.

EVENING SNACK

DAY 4

BREAKFAST:
1 cup low-fat cottage cheese
1 cup pineapple
1 orange
3 macadamia nuts
Mix together and enjoy.

LUNCH:
1 soy burger patty
2 oz. reduced-fat cheese
lettuce and tomato slice
dill pickle wedge (optional)
1 teaspoon reduced-fat mayonnaise
1 side salad
1 Tablespoon olive oil & vinegar dressing

1 1/3 cup unsweetened applesauce, sprinkled
with cinnamon
*Spray nonstick pan with vegetable spray. Cook
soy burger according to package instructions.*

AFTERNOON SNACK

DINNER:
4 oz. chicken breast, no skin
lemon slices
onion slices
1 to 2 teaspoons barbecue sauce
2 cups green beans sauteed in garlic with
4 teaspoons slivered almonds
1 apple
*Preheat oven to 450° F. Cover chicken breast
with slices of onion and lemon. Bake for 15 minutes. Reduce heat to 350° F. Baste with barbecue
sauce. Cook for 10 to 15 minutes or until done.*

EVENING SNACK

DAY 5

BREAKFAST:
8 egg white omelette with 2 teaspoons of olive
oil and 1/2 cup of spinach and mushrooms
1 cup slow-cooked oatmeal
1 cup strawberries

LUNCH:
   chicken Caesar salad with 4 oz. of chicken
   3 cups steamed vegetables
   1 pear

AFTERNOON SNACK

DINNER:
   7 oz. grilled salmon
   small garden salad
   4 cups steamed vegetables
   1/4 cup chickpeas
   1 cup of fruit

EVENING SNACK

Zone Snacks

You can create your own snacks by choosing one item from each food group below. Remember, to be a Zone snack, you need one each of protein, carbohydrate and fat.

Proteins:
   1/4 cup 2% cottage cheese
   1 oz. cheese, part skim or low-fat
   1 mozzarella stick (1 oz), part skim or 'lite'
   1 1/2 oz. sliced deli meat (turkey, ham, etc.)
   1 oz. tuna

Carbohydrates:

1/2 apple
1/2 cup grapes
1/2 orange
1/2 pear
1/2 grapefruit
1 plum
1 peach
1 tangerine
1 kiwi
1/4 cantaloupe
1/2 cup blueberries
1 cup strawberries
3/4 cup blackberries
8 cherries
2/3 cup honeydew melon
3/4 cup watermelon

Fats:

3 olives
1 macadamia nut
1/4 inch slice of avocado
3 almonds
6 peanuts
2 pecan halves

Now you can put together your own 30-day plan, one bite at a time, using your own favorite recipes — sticking to low-carb ingredients of course — or with some of these delicious dishes provided courtesy of several of America's food producer groups.

But it's time for a quick — and critical — word on liquid refreshment. And we don't mean martinis.

Believe it or not, one of the best weapons you have in your battle of the bulge is water. Most experts recommend 8 glasses a day. And scientific studies show drinking water in proper amounts can actually cause fat deposits to shrink.

Why? The kidneys need plenty of water to work the way they should. When the water isn't there, they begin pushing some of their work off onto the liver, which then can't completely perform its own task of metabolizing fat. Result: more fat stays in the body and you begin to hate mirrors.

But there's more. When your body isn't getting enough water, it's programmed to prepare for a threatening shortage of life-sustaining liquid by warehousing what it does get, instead of excreting any surplus as waste. And where is it stored? In your arms and legs, hands and feet, which then begin to swell, sometimes painfully, always with an unsightly result. Increasing your intake will end the problem.

Water supports the muscles. It hydrates the

skin. It helps the kidneys remove poisons from the body and the bowels to remove solid waste. It really is the stuff of life.

And it's especially important to those trying to lose weight — if you get enough of it, at least eight glasses a day; more if you are overweight and trying to lose a substantial number of pounds. Your diet will cause your body to metabolize fat, generating more waste that the water will help you get rid. As the fat cells disappear, they will leave tiny pockets in your skin. Water will fill them, keeping your skin from sagging as the fat disappears.

Now, on with the low-carb feast. You can begin the journey back to a low-fat body with the recipes on the following pages.

PORK

(Recipes Courtesy National Pork Board)

While standard American-raised pork is not as fatty as people believe, like all meat it does have some fat. You don't want to eat that in your new Ultimate lifestyle, so trim it away before you cook the meat.

HERBED BUTTERFLY PORK CHOPS

> 4 boneless butterfly pork chops, about 4 ounces each
> 2 tablespoons lemon juice
> 2 tablespoons chopped parsley
> 1/2 teaspoon crumbled rosemary
> 1/2 teaspoon crumbled thyme
> 1/4 teaspoon black pepper

Brush chops with lemon juice. Combine remaining ingredients; mix well. Rub herb mixture on both sides of chops. Grill or broil for 10-12 minutes, turning occasionally. Garnish with fresh herbs, if desired. *Serves 4.*

Nutrition Information Per Serving: Calories, 149; carbs, 1

PEPPERED PORK TENDERLOIN

> 1 whole pork tenderloin, about 1 pound

2 teaspoons lemon pepper
1/2 teaspoon cayenne (red pepper) OR pepper blend seasoning

Rub tenderloin with both pepper seasonings, covering entire surface. Place in shallow roasting pan and roast in 425° F oven for 15-20 minutes, until internal temperature (measured with a meat thermometer) reads 155-160° F. Let roast rest for 5 minutes before slicing to serve. *Serves 4.*

Nutrition Information Per Serving: calories, 140; carbs, 1

GRILLED CHIMICHURRI PORK ROAST

3-pound boneless pork roast
1 cup coarsely chopped parsley
1/4 cup chopped onion
6 garlic cloves, coarsely chopped
1/4 cup lemon juice
1/4 cup olive oil
1 teaspoon dried oregano
1 teaspoon crushed red pepper
1 teaspoon salt
1/2 teaspoon black pepper
Lemon slices, for garnish
Lime slices, for garnish

Place pork roast in self-sealing plastic bag. In

food processor, place parsley, onion and garlic and pulse until minced. Add remaining ingredients, except garnish, and process to blend. Coat pork in plastic bag with this mixture. Seal bag and refrigerate overnight. Prepare medium-hot fire in grill. Remove pork from marinade (discard marinade) and place pork roast over drip pan on grill over indirect heat. Close grill cover and cook until internal temperature (measured with a meat thermometer) reads 155° F, about 45 minutes to an hour. Let stand 10 minutes before slicing. Garnish with lemon and lime slices. *Serves 12.*

Nutrition Information Per Serving: Calories, 170; carbs, 0

LEAN HOMEMADE
BREAKFAST SAUSAGE

1 pound lean ground pork
1/2 teaspoon ground rosemary
1/8 teaspoon ground thyme
1/8 teaspoon dried marjoram, crushed
1/8 teaspoon pepper
1/8 teaspoon salt

Combine all ingredients; mix well. Place in an air-tight container. Chill in the refrigerator 4 to 24 hours to allow flavors to blend. Shape into 1/2-inch thick patties. In skillet, cook patties over medium heat about 4-5 minutes on each side, or until done. TO BROIL: Place patties on an unheated rack in broiler pan. Broil 5 inches from heat about 5 minutes on each side. *Serves 8.*

Nutrition Information Per Serving: Calories, 120; carbs, 0

QUICK-CURED PORK LOIN

3-pound boneless pork loin roast
1/4 cup vegetable oil
3 cloves garlic, minced
2 tablespoons coarse salt

Place roast in large (2-gallon) self-sealing bag. Add oil, garlic and salt, and rub over pork, coating roast well. Seal bag and refrigerate 2 to 24 hours. Remove pork from marinade (discard any remaining marinade) and place on grill. Lower grill hood and grill for 1 to 1 1/4 hours, until internal temperature is 155° F (measured with a meat thermometer). Remove to serving platter and let stand 10 minutes. Serve sliced. *Serves 8.*

Nutrition Information Per Serving: Calories, 270; carbs, 0

GRILLED LEG OF PORK

4-pound boneless leg of pork
3/4 cup chili sauce

1/4 cup red wine vinegar
2 tablespoons lemon juice
1 teaspoon dry mustard
1 clove garlic, minced

Prepare medium-hot banked fire in covered kettle-style grill. Place pork over indirect heat, cover grill and grill for 1 1/2-2 hours, until internal temperature (measured with a meat thermometer) registers 150-155° F. Meanwhile, in a small bowl combine chili sauce, vinegar, lemon juice, mustard and garlic; mix well. Brush pork frequently with sauce during the last hour of grilling time. Let pork rest for 10 minutes before slicing to serve. *Serves 8-12.*

Nutrition Information Per Serving: Calories, 390 ; carbs, 1

JERK PORK CHOPS

6 4-ounce boneless center-cut loin pork chops, about 1/2-inch thick
1-1/2 teaspoons ground allspice
3/4 teaspoons salt
1 teaspoon dried thyme
1 teaspoon ground coriander
1 teaspoon cinnamon
1 teaspoon nutmeg
1 teaspoon garlic powder

1/4 teaspoon cayenne pepper
2 tablespoons vegetable oil

Combine all seasonings and oil in a small bowl; mix to blend. Spread paste mixture on both sides of each pork chop. Place pork chops in a self-sealing plastic bag or baking dish and cover. Chill for several hours or overnight in refrigerator. Place chops on rack in broiler pan; broil 4 to 5 inches from heat for 5 to 6 minutes on each side, until brown and chops reach an internal temperature of 160° F (measured with a meat thermometer). *Serves 6.*

Nutrition Information Per Serving: calories, 170; carbs, 2

CARIBBEAN-STYLE PORK RIB CHOPS (COSTILLITAS DE CERDO)

6 pork rib chops, about 1-inch thick
4 garlic cloves
1 bay leaf
1 teaspoon oregano
1 teaspoon salt
1/2 cup dry white wine
1/4 cup bitter orange juice * (recipe follows)
1 tablespoon lard or oil

Place pork chops in a glass baking dish or other non-metal dish. In a food processor or blender, combine garlic, bay leaf, oregano, salt, wine and juice; process until well blended. Pour over chops, turning to coat all sides. Cover and allow to marinate for up to one hour, turning once or twice. In large skillet heat 1 tablespoon of lard or oil. Blot pork chops with paper towels and sauté until brown on both sides, about 4 minutes on each side. *Serves 6*.

Nutrition Information Per Serving: Calories, 165; carbs, 2

BITTER ORANGE SUBSTITUTE

> 2 tablespoons fresh grapefruit juice
> 2 tablespoons fresh orange juice
> 1/4 cup fresh lime juice

Mix everything together thoroughly about 1 hour before using. Keep in the refrigerator, tightly sealed, no more than 3 or 4 days. Makes about 1/2 cup.

CAROLINA COUNTRY-STYLE RIBS

> 1 1/2 to 2 pounds boneless country-style ribs
> 2 cups apple cider vinegar
> 1 cup cold water
> 2 tablespoons vegetable oil
> 2 tablespoons molasses or 1/4 cup firmly packed
>   brown sugar
> 1 tablespoon Kosher salt

   1 1/2 teaspoons red pepper flakes
   1/2 teaspoon cayenne pepper

Place ribs in a large bowl or resealable plastic bag, set aside. In 4-cup glass measure, stir together vinegar, water, oil, molasses, salt, red pepper flakes and cayenne pepper until salt is dissolved. Remove 1/2 cup marinade; set aside. Add remaining marinade to ribs; seal bag and marinate for 4 to 6 hours in the refrigerator. Remove ribs from marinade; discard marinade.

Prepare medium-hot fire; grill ribs over indirect heat for 50 to 60 minutes or until pork is tender and the internal temperature reaches 160° F (measured with a meat thermometer). Baste ribs twice with reserved sauce mixture during last 15 minutes of grilling. *Serves 6.*

Nutrition Information Per Serving: calories, 232; carbs, 2

GRILLED HONEY-SOY PORK STEAKS

   2 pork blade steaks, cut 1-inch thick
   2 small cloves garlic, minced
   2 tablespoons finely chopped onion
   2 tablespoon lemon juice
   2 tablespoon soy sauce
   1 tablespoon honey

Combine all ingredients in a self-sealing plastic bag; seal bag and place in refrigerator 4 to 24 hours. Remove steaks from marinade, discarding marinade. Grill over medium-hot coals, 7 minutes per side, turning once. *Serves 4.*

Nutrition Information Per Serving: calories, 260; carbs, 2

SAUSAGE SPROUT OMELET

    4 sausage links
    4 eggs, slightly beaten
    2 tablespoons milk
    1/4 teaspoon celery salt
    1/8 teaspoon pepper
    2 tablespoons butter or margarine
    1/4 cup shredded Cheddar cheese (1 ounce)
    1/4 cup fresh bean sprouts
    Optional garnishes: Fresh dillweed, fresh strawberries, sliced kiwi fruit, sliced nectarines, lettuce leaves

Cook sausage links over medium heat until done, turning occasionally. Cut into 1/2-inch pieces and set aside. Combine eggs, milk, celery salt and pepper in a small bowl; beat with whisk until well mixed, but not frothy. Heat 1 tablespoon butter in 8-inch omelet pan over medium-high heat. Pour in half of egg mixture. Cook, gently lifting edges with a spatula so uncooked mixture flows underneath. When eggs are

almost set, sprinkle half of the omelet with half
the cheese, half the sausage and half the sprouts.
Fold omelet; turn onto serving plate. Repeat
with remaining ingredients. If desired, garnish
with dillweed and fruit on lettuce leaf. *Serves 2.*

Nutrition Information Per Serving: calories, 414; carbs, 3

NORTH BEACH PORK BOCCONCINI

2 pounds boneless pork loin, cut into 3/4-inch
    cubes
3/4 cup cider vinegar
3/4 cup olive oil
4 tablespoons lemon juice
1 tablespoon Worcestershire sauce
1 tablespoon oregano
1 teaspoon thyme
2 garlic cloves, minced
2 teaspoons black pepper
1 teaspoon salt
1/2 teaspoon cayenne

Place all ingredients in a 1-gallon self-sealing
plastic bag, mix well. Seal bag and marinate in the
refrigerator 8 to 12 hours or overnight. Heat oven
to 350° F. Remove pork cubes from marinade, discarding marinade. Pat pork dry with paper towels;
place cubes in a single layer, not touching, in a
shallow baking pan and bake at 350° F for 25-30

minutes, until pork is just tender and lightly browned. Remove to serving platter or chafing dish and serve hot. *Serves 16. Cut all ingredients proportionate to number being served.*

Nutrition information based on 1/4 marinade: calories, 94; carbs 0

SWEET & SOUR PORK MEATBALLS

1 pound lean ground pork
1/4 cup finely chopped water chestnuts
1/4 cup chopped onion
1 egg, slightly beaten
2 tablespoons soy sauce
1/8 teaspoon ground ginger
1 teaspoon vegetable oil
1 8-ounce can pineapple chunks
2 tablespoons soy sauce
1 tablespoon vinegar
1 tablespoon cornstarch
1 tablespoon sugar

In a large mixing bowl mix together pork, water chestnuts, onion, egg, 2 tablespoons soy sauce and ginger; shape into 1-inch balls. In a large nonstick skillet cook meatballs in remaining 2 Tablespoons of hot oil until browned, turning to brown evenly. Drain pineapple, reserving juice. In a 1-cup measure combine pineapple juice, 2 tablespoons soy sauce and vinegar. Add water to make 1 cup liquid. In mixing bowl combine cornstarch and sugar. Gradually stir in pineapple juice mixture; mix thoroughly. Add juice mixture to pan drippings. Cook over medium heat until thickened and bubbly, stirring constantly. Stir in meatballs and the reserved pineapple. Cook for 4 to 5 minutes or until heated through. *Serves 24.*

Nutrition Information Per Serving: calories, 41; carbs, 3

RALEIGH-DURHAM PORK BARBECUE

1 quart cider vinegar
1 tablespoon crushed red pepper
1 tablespoon black pepper
4-pound boneless pork shoulder (Boston Butt)

Stir together vinegar and peppers. Prepare medium-hot coals in covered grill, banking coals when hot. Position drip pan in center of grill bed, between banks of coals. Place pork on grill over drip pan, close hood. Cook for 2 1/2 to 3 1/2 hours, basting frequently with vinegar marinade, until pork is very tender. Remove pork from grill, cool slightly; chop meat and serve. *Serves 16.*

Nutrition Information Per Serving: calories, 178; carbs, 4

MASITAS DE CERDO (CARNITAS)

1 1/2 pounds boneless pork loin, cut into 1-inch
　　cubes
6 garlic cloves, crushed
1 teaspoon salt
1/2 teaspoon black pepper
1 teaspoon oregano
1/4 cup olive oil
1/2 cup sour orange juice (or use 1/4 cup orange
　　juice and 1/4 cup lime juice)

Place pork cubes in a self-sealing plastic
bag; mix together remaining ingredients and
pour over pork cubes; seal bag and refrigerate
overnight. Remove pork from marinade, discarding marinade, and place pork cubes in a
shallow baking pan. Roast in a 350° F oven
for 25 to 30 minutes, until pork is tender.
Remove to serving platter and serve hot.
Serves 6.

Nutrition Information Per Serving: calories, 233; carbs, 3

ROASTED PORK TENDERLOIN WITH OREGANO-CORIANDER RUB

1 pork tenderloin, about 1 pound
1 teaspoon dried oregano, crushed
1 teaspoon ground coriander

1/2 teaspoon dried thyme, crushed
1/2 teaspoon ground cumin
1/2 teaspoon curry powder
1/4 teaspoon coarse salt
2 tablespoons chopped fresh flat-leaf parsley

Trim any fat from pork. For dry rub, combine oregano, coriander, thyme, cumin, curry powder and salt in small bowl. Moisten pork tenderloin with water; coat with dry rub. If desired, place pork in shallow dish; cover and marinate in refrigerator for 8 hours or overnight. Heat oven to 450° F. Place pork on rack in shallow roasting pan. Roast until an instant-read meat thermometer inserted into center of pork reads 160° F, 25 to 30 minutes. Remove from oven. Slice pork; arrange slices on a serving plate. Sprinkle with parsley. *Serves 4.*
Nutrition Information Per Serving: calories, 138; carbs 1

ITALIAN PORK SPIEDINI

1 pork tenderloin, about 1 pound, cut into 1/2-inch
   cubes
1 cup Italian salad dressing

Marinade pork in salad dressing for 30 minutes. Thread pork on skewers* and discard marinade. Grill for 10 to 12 minutes, turning occasionally, until done. *Serves 4.*

*Note: If using bamboo skewers, soak in water for at least 30 minutes to prevent burning.

Nutrition Information Per Serving: calories, 180; carbs, 1

QUICK-MIX BREAKFAST SAUSAGE

1 teaspoon ground sage
1/2 teaspoon dried savory
1/4 teaspoon ground black pepper
1/4 teaspoon nutmeg
1/2 teaspoon salt
1 pound ground pork

Thoroughly mix pork and seasonings. May refrigerate covered to allow flavors to blend. Shape into patties and brown OR crumble and brown for use in a recipe. *Serves 8.*

Note: For Spiced Breakfast Sausage: To Breakfast Sausage mix add 1/4 teaspoon EACH ground cloves and ground mace.

Nutrition Information Per Serving: calories, 120; carbs, 1

<u>EGGS</u>

(Recipes Courtesy of the American Egg Board)

TIP: Whenever possible use omega-3 enriched eggs, now available in many well-stocked supermarkets, some low-carb authorities suggest. They are sold under various product names, but they all have in common higher levels of the polyunsaturated fats called omega-3s, which also are found in fish, fish oils, canola oil, soybean and flax seed. Scientists have shown that omega-3s can help cut the risk of heart disease. Omega-3 enriched eggs are produced by giving laying hens special diets that contain 10 percent to 20 percent ground flax seed.

QUICHE FLORENTINE

6 eggs, divided
1/2 teaspoon garlic powder, divided
1/4 cup grated Parmesan cheese
1/2 cup orzo (rice-shaped pasta), cooked and drained
1/2 cup skim or low-fat milk
1 teaspoon Italian seasoning, crushed
10-ounce package frozen chopped spinach, thawed, drained and pressed

2 ounce-can sliced mushrooms
drained nectarine slices, optional

In medium bowl, beat together 1 egg, 1/4 teaspoon garlic powder and the cheese. Stir in orzo until well blended. To form crust, spread orzo mixture over bottom and up sides of lightly greased deep 9-inch quiche dish or pie plate. Beat together remaining eggs, remaining garlic powder, milk and seasoning until well blended. Stir in spinach and mushrooms until well combined. Pour into prepared crust. Bake in preheated 375° F oven until puffed in center and knife inserted near center comes out clean, about 30 to 40 minutes. Let stand 5 minutes before serving. Garnish with nectarine slices, if desired. *Makes 6 servings.*

Nutrition Information Per Serving of 1/6 recipe using skim milk without optional ingredients: calories, 173; carbs, 17

ITALIAN TIDBITS

6 eggs
1/2 cup non-fat or low-fat (1%) milk
1 cup all-purpose flour
1/4 cup grated Parmesan cheese
1/2 teaspoon baking powder
1/2 teaspoon garlic salt
Cooking spray

> 1/3 cup bottled pizza sauce
> 2.25 ounce-can sliced ripe olives, drained
> 1/2 cup chopped sweet red or green pepper
> 1/4 cup chopped green onions with tops
> 1/2 cup (2 ounces) shredded low-moisture part-skim mozzarella cheese

In medium bowl or covered blender container, beat together or blend eggs and milk until blended. In small bowl, stir together flour, Parmesan cheese, baking powder and garlic salt. Add to egg mixture. Beat or cover and blend until smooth. Pour into spray coated 12 x 7 1/2 x 2-inch baking dish. Dollop small spoonfuls of pizza sauce over top. Draw fork through batter, swirling sauce into batter. Sprinkle with olives, pepper and onions. Bake in preheated 325° F oven 20 minutes. Sprinkle with cheese. Bake until knife inserted in center comes out clean, about an additional 5 to 10 minutes. Cut diagonally to form triangles. Serve hot or chill to serve cold. *Makes 32 bite-size pieces — or 6 to 8 appetizer servings.*

Nutrition Information Per Serving of 1/8 recipe using skim milk and green pepper: calories, 165; carbs, 15

CAULIFLOWER FRITTATA

> 1 1/2 cups sliced fresh cauliflower florets (about 10 ounces)*

1/2 cup water
Cooking spray
2 eggs
1/4 cup reduced-fat mayonnaise
1 tablespoon chopped chives
1/4 teaspoon dry mustard
Dash salt, optional
2 tablespoons (0.5 ounce) shredded reduced-fat
        Cheddar cheese, optional

In medium saucepan, bring cauliflower and water to boil. Reduce heat. Cover. Simmer until crisp-tender, about 5 to 10 minutes. Drain. Evenly coat 8-inch omelet pan or skillet with spray. Add drained cauliflower florets. In small bowl, beat together eggs, mayonnaise, chives, mustard and salt, if desired, until blended. Pour over cauliflower florets. Cook over medium heat until eggs are almost set, about 8 to 10 minutes. Sprinkle with cheese. Cover pan. Remove from heat. Let stand until no visible liquid egg remains and cheese is melted, about 3 to 5 minutes. Slide from pan onto serving plate. Cut in half or into wedges. *Or use 1 package (10 ounces) frozen chopped cauliflower. Thaw or cook according to package directions. *Makes 2 servings.*

Nutrition Information Per Serving of 1/2 recipe without optional salt and cheese: calories, 136; carbs, 7

And, of course, there are my favorites: eggs scrambled or fried in bacon fat; two make a great breakfast, especially with a couple of strips of bacon or 2 sausage patties.

CHICKEN

(Recipes courtesy National Chicken Council/U.S. Poultry & Egg Association)

Chicken contains some fat, particularly in the skin. So trim all that away; remove the skin and any bright yellow globs of fat you find on the meat before cooking.

HEALTHFUL CHICKEN CASSEROLE

1 broiler-fryer chicken, cooked, skinned, chopped
10 ounces frozen spinach
1/4 cup finely chopped onion
1/2 teaspoon garlic powder, divided
8 ounces fresh mushrooms, sliced
2 tablespoons margarine, melted
1 cup low-fat mozzarella cheese

Cook spinach according to package directions, eliminating salt; drain. Mix onions with spinach. Arrange spinach in bottom of 1 1/2-quart baking dish; sprinkle with 1/4 teaspoon of the garlic powder. Arrange mushrooms on spinach and drizzle with melted margarine. Place chicken on mushrooms and sprinkle with remaining 1/4 teaspoon of the garlic powder. Top with mozzarella cheese. Place in 350° F oven and bake for 30 minutes. *Makes 6 servings.*

Nutrition Information Per Serving: calories, 202; carbs, 4

STIR-FRY CHICKEN WITH VEGETABLES

- 1-1/2 pounds boneless, skinless chicken thighs, cut in thin slices
- 1-1/2 cups small cauliflower florets
- 1-1/2 cups small broccoli florets
- 1 cup thinly sliced carrots
- 1 cup sliced green onion, tops included
- 1 teaspoon salt
- 1/4 teaspoon pepper
- 1/2 cup chicken broth, heated

Preheat heavy frypan about 3 minutes on medium-high heat; spray with nonstick corn oil cooking spray. Add chicken slices and stir-fry about 3 minutes. Increase heat to high and add cauliflower, broccoli and carrots; continue to stir-fry about 3 minutes. Add onion, salt and pepper, continuing to stir-fry about 3 minutes more. Add warm chicken broth, scraping drippings from bottom of frypan, and cook about 2 minutes more. Serve alone or with cooked thin spaghetti or rice. *Makes 4 servings.*

Nutrition Information Per Serving: calories, 309; carbs, 10.2

CHICKEN AND SPINACH MEDLEY

1 tablespoon canola oil
1 clove garlic, minced
4 boneless, skinless chicken breast halves
1/2 cup low-sodium chicken broth
1/2 cup green pepper slivers
1 medium onion, cut into thin rings
4 ounce-can mushroom slices
2 bunches fresh spinach (about 1 1/2 pounds)
1/2 teaspoon salt
1/4 teaspoon pepper
3 tablespoons grated Romano cheese
1 cup fresh bread croutons

In nonstick frypan, place oil and heat to medium temperature. Add garlic, stirring to spread evenly in frypan. Arrange chicken in single layer over garlic and cook about 5 minutes; turn and cook 5 minutes more. In large frypan, pour chicken broth and heat on high temperature. Add green pepper, onion and mushrooms;

cook 3 minutes. Add spinach and cook, stirring with other vegetables, about 2 minutes more. Turn off heat under vegetables. Remove chicken from small frypan and cut into strips. Add chicken strips to vegetables in large frypan; stir to mix well. Sprinkle with salt and pepper. Remove to serving dish and top with cheese and croutons. *Makes 4 servings.*

Nutrition Information Per Serving: calories, 267; carbs, 13.2

CAJUN CHICKEN BREASTS

4 boneless, skinless chicken breasts
1/4 teaspoon cayenne pepper
2 cloves garlic, minced
1/4 teaspoon dried mint
1 tablespoon fresh, finely chopped parsley
2 tablespoons white wine
vegetable cooking spray
1/4 teaspoon salt

In shallow refrigerator dish with cover, mix together garlic, parsley, salt, cayenne pepper and mint; stir in wine. Spread mixture on all sides of chicken breasts, cover and refrigerate at least 3 hours or overnight. At cooking time, spray nonstick frypan with vegetable cooking spray. Heat over medium-high temperature about 1 minute, add chicken and cook about 5 minutes. Turn chicken and cook another 5 minutes. *Makes 4 servings.*

Nutrition Information Per Serving: calories, 145; carbs, 0.7

GRILLED CHICKEN BREASTS WITH SPICY SALSA

- 6 chicken breast halves
- 4 tablespoons fresh lime juice
- 1/4 cup olive oil
- 1/2 teaspoon chili powder
- 1/4 teaspoon pepper
- Spicy Salsa: recipe follows
- 1 avocado, peeled, pitted, sliced into wedges
- 1 tablespoon finely chopped cilantro

In shallow glass dish, mix together lime juice, olive oil, chili powder and pepper. Add chicken, turning to coat. Cover and marinate in refrigerator at least 1 hour. Place chicken on prepared grill, skin side down, at least 8 inches from heat.* Grill about 8 minutes, turn chicken and grill about 8 minutes more or until fork can be inserted in chicken with ease and juices run clear, not pink. Remove chicken to serving platter. Spoon Spicy Salsa over each piece and garnish with avocado wedges. Sprinkle with cilantro. *Makes 6 servings.*

Nutrition Information Per Serving: calories, 285; carbs, 15.2

*Note: Chicken may be broiled instead of grilled. Place on broiler pan, skin side down; broil about 10 minutes, turn and broil about 10 minutes more or until fork tender.

SPICY SALSA

In medium bowl, mix together 3 medium red or yellow tomatoes (seeded and chopped), 1/4 cup finely chopped red onion, 1 tablespoon fresh lime juice, 1 large clove garlic (minced), 2 teaspoons seeded and minced jalapeno pepper, 2 tablespoons finely chopped cilantro, 1/4 teaspoon ground cumin and 1/2 teaspoon salt. Let sit at room temperature about 1 hour.

QUICK CORIANDER CHICKEN BREASTS

4 boneless, skinless chicken breast halves
3 tablespoons light soy sauce
1 tablespoon coriander seeds, crushed
1 tablespoon red wine vinegar
1 teaspoon brown sugar
2 cloves garlic, minced
1/4 teaspoon poultry seasoning
1/2 teaspoon coarsely ground pepper
1 tablespoon olive oil

Place soy sauce, crushed coriander seeds, vine-

gar, brown sugar, garlic and poultry seasoning in
food processor container and process 1 minute.
Place chicken breasts in shallow bowl; pour sauce
over chicken and turn to coat well. Sprinkle with
pepper. In frypan, place olive oil and heat to
medium temperature. Add chicken and cook,
turning, about 7 minutes per side or until fork can
be inserted with ease. Pour any remaining sauce
over chicken after first turning. *Makes 4 serving.*

Nutrition Information Per Serving: calories, 172; carbs, 3.2

SPANISH OLIVE CHICKEN

        1 broiler-fryer cut-up chicken
        3 tablespoons olive oil
        1 teaspoon salt
        1 teaspoon cinnamon
        1/4 teaspoon pepper
        3 large tomatoes, each cut in 6 wedges
        1/2 cup sliced black olives
        1/2 cup white wine
        3 tablespoons tomato paste

In large heavy frypan or Dutch oven, place
olive oil and heat over medium-high temperature. Add chicken and cook, turning, about 10
minutes or until brown on all sides. Drain off oil
and discard. Mix together salt, cinnamon and
pepper; sprinkle on all sides of chicken in pan.

Add tomatoes and olives; pour wine over all. Cover and simmer on low heat about 40 minutes or until fork can be inserted in chicken with ease. Remove chicken to warm serving bowl. Add tomato paste to ingredients in pan; bring to a boil over high heat and cook, uncovered, about 1 minute more. Pour sauce over chicken. *Makes 4 servings.*

Nutrition Information Per Serving: calories, 465; carbs, 13.7

VIETNAMESE CHICKEN IN TOMATO SAUCE

1 1/4 pounds boneless, skinless chicken breast, cut into strips

1/8 teaspoon black pepper

2 tablespoons cooking oil

1/2 cup Spanish-style tomato sauce

2 green onions, white and green parts included, cut into 1-inch pieces

1/2 cup water

1 1/2 tablespoons fish sauce

8 ounce-can bamboo shoots, drained, rinsed

2 tablespoons toasted sesame seeds, crushed

1/2 teaspoon garlic salt

In medium bowl, mix together chicken, green onion, bamboo shoots, garlic salt and pepper; cover and refrigerate about 15 minutes. In frypan, place oil and heat over medium temperature. Add chicken mixture and cook, stirring, about 10 minutes or until pink is gone from chicken. In small bowl, mix together tomato sauce, water and fish sauce; pour over chicken. Raise heat to medium-high and bring to a boil. Cover, reduce heat to low and cook about 10 minutes more. Sprinkle with crushed sesame seeds and serve with rice or Chinese noodles. *Makes 6 servings.*

Nutrition Information Per Serving: calories, 239; carbs, 3.9

PASTA

(Recipes courtesy of Dreamfields Healthy Low-Carb Living Pasta)

BAKED PENNE PASTA WITH TOMATOES AND MOZZARELLA

16 ounces Dreamfields low-carb penne pasta (or elbow macaroni)
3 tablespoons olive oil
1 teaspoon minced garlic
15-ounce can diced tomatoes, drained
Salt and pepper, to taste
8 ounces shredded mozzarella

Cook the pasta according to the package directions. Preheat the oven to 375° F. Meanwhile, heat the oil in a heavy skillet. Stir in the garlic and cook 1 minute. Stir in the tomatoes and cook 2 minutes longer. Season to taste with salt and pepper. Toss the tomato mixture with the pasta. Pour into a well greased 2-quart shallow casserole. Top with the cheese. Place in the preheated oven and bake for 10 to 15 minutes or until the cheese is melted. *Makes 8 servings.*

Nutrition Information Per Serving: calories, 369; carbs, 10

LINGUINE PUTTANESCA

   16 ounces Dreamfields low-carb linguine
   1/4 cup extra-virgin olive oil
   3 large cloves garlic
   1/2 cup chopped yellow onion
   1/2 to 1 teaspoon crushed red chili peppers
   1/2 teaspoon salt, or to taste
   28-ounce can Italian plum tomatoes, diced
   2/3 cup kalamata olives, halved
   1 cup freshly grated Parmesan cheese

Cook the pasta according to package directions. Meanwhile, heat the oil in a large skillet. Add the garlic and onion and cook, stirring, for about 3 minutes. Stir in the red pepper and salt. Add the tomatoes and cook over high heat for 5 minutes, stirring often. Stir in olives and cook 5 minutes more. Taste and correct the seasonings. Drain the cooked pasta well. Toss into the sauce. Sprinkle with cheese to serve. *Makes 6 servings.*

Nutrition Information Per Serving: calories, 481; carbs, 16

SPAGHETTI WITH PROSCIUTTO AND ASPARAGUS

- 16 ounces Dreamfields low-carb spaghetti
- 8 ounces fresh asparagus
- 1 tablespoon olive oil
- 1 clove garlic, minced
- 1 medium onion, chopped (1/2 cup)
- 2 ounces prosciutto, chopped
- 4 tablespoons chopped fresh parsley
- 2 cups whipping cream
- 1/2 teaspoon salt
- 1/2 teaspoon pepper
- 1 teaspoon nutmeg
- 1 cup Parmesan cheese

Wash asparagus and cut into 1-inch pieces. Discard bottoms. Heat oil in 12-inch skillet over medium heat. Saute garlic and onion in oil for 3 to 5 minutes, stirring occasionally. Add prosciutto and parsley and cook 3 more minutes. Stir in cream and add asparagus; season with salt, pepper and nutmeg. Heat to boiling, reduce heat to low and simmer for 10 minutes, stirring occasionally. Meanwhile, cook pasta according to package directions. Drain well and toss in bowl with sauce. Top with Parmesan cheese and serve. Garnish individual servings with additional Parmesan cheese and fresh cracked black pepper. *Makes 6 servings.*

Nutrition Information Per Serving: calories, 626; carbs, 14

SOUTHWEST PASTA SALAD

- 16 ounces Dreamfields low-carb penne or elbow macaroni
- 1 cup cherry or grape tomatoes, halved
- 1 red bell pepper, cut into small strips
- 2 to 3 jalapeno peppers, minced
- 1 large sweet salad onion, halved and thinly sliced
- 1 to 2 ripe avocados, diced
- 1/4 cup chopped cilantro
- 1 cup mayonnaise
- 1 cup tomato salsa
- 1 tablespoon fresh lime juice
- 1 teaspoon salt

Cook the pasta according to directions. Drain and quickly rinse with cool water. Set aside to drain thoroughly. Place the drained pasta in a large serving bowl and add the tomatoes, bell pepper, jalapenos, onion slices, avocados and cilantro. Toss lightly just to mix. To make the dressing: Whisk together mayonnaise, salsa, lime juice and salt. Toss into the pasta mixture. Serve immediately or cover and chill until ready to serve. *Makes 10 servings.*

Nutrition Information Per Serving: calories, 368; carbs, 10

ELBOW MACARONI SALAD

    16 ounces Dreamfields low-carb elbow macaroni
    1 cup sour cream
    1/2 cup mayonnaise
    1/2 cup chopped fresh parsley
    1 tablespoon lemon juice
    1/2 teaspoon salt
    1/2 teaspoon pepper
    1/2 cup chopped green onion
    1 cup cucumber, diced 1/2 -inch thick
    1 cup broccoli florets
    1/4 cup carrot, chopped

Prepare pasta according to package directions. Rinse under cold water and drain well. Mix together sour cream, mayonnaise, parsley, lemon juice, salt and pepper. Combine dressing with vegetables. Add pasta and toss gently with other ingredients until well coated. Refrigerate at least 1 hour prior to serving. *Makes 10 servings.*

Nutrition Information Per Serving: calories, 234; carbs, 5

THAI-STYLE PENNE

16 ounces Dreamfields penne rigate
3 tablespoons peanut oil
2 tablespoons chopped fresh mint leaves
2 small Thai peppers, minced
1 tablespoon fresh cilantro leaves plus
    1 tablespoon for garnish
1/2 cup diced cucumber (1/3-inch dice)
1/2 cup hearts of palm in brine, drained
2 tablespoons unsalted chopped peanuts, divided
1 teaspoon lemon zest
3 tablespoons water
2 tablespoons soy sauce
1 tablespoon lemon juice

Cook pasta according to package directions. Meanwhile, heat oil in 12-inch skillet over medium heat. Cook mint, peppers and cilantro 3 minutes, stirring often. Add cucumber, hearts of palm, 1 tablespoon chopped peanuts and lemon zest. Pour in water, soy sauce and lemon juice. Cover and cook 5 minutes. Drain pasta and add to pan. Toss well and cook 3 minutes longer over high heat. Top with garnish of cilantro and peanuts. *Makes 6 servings.*

Nutrition Information Per Serving: calories, 353; carbs, 10

BEEF

(Recipes courtesy Cattlemen's Beef Board)

Always buy the leanest beef you can find, preferably grass-fed, if it's available. Trim off any fat around the edges. There are no carbs in beef, but there can be plenty of fat. In preparing your menu plan, you should try to keep fats, as well as carbs, as low as you can.

BURGUNDY BEEF & VEGETABLE STEW

1-1/2 pounds beef for stew, cut in 1-inch pieces
1 tablespoon vegetable oil
1 teaspoon dried thyme
1/2 teaspoon salt
1/2 teaspoon pepper
13-3/4 to 14-1/2 ounce-can ready-to-serve beef
   broth
1/2 cup Burgundy wine
3 large cloves garlic, minced
1-1/2 cups baby carrots
1 cup frozen whole pearl onions
2 tablespoons cornstarch dissolved in
   2 tablespoons water
8 ounce-package frozen sugar snap peas

Heat oil in Dutch oven over medium heat

until hot. Brown beef in batches; pour off drippings. Return beef to pan; season with thyme, salt and pepper. Stir in broth, wine and garlic; bring to a boil. Reduce heat; cover tightly and simmer 1-1/4 hours. Stir in carrots and onions; continue cooking, covered, 30 to 45 minutes or until beef and vegetables are tender. Stir in cornstarch mixture; cook and stir 1 minute or until thickened. Stir in sugar snap peas. Cook 3 to 4 minutes or until heated through. *Makes 6 servings.*

Nutrition Information Per Serving: calories, 239; carbs, 15

GRILLED BEEF SIRLOIN & FARMERS MARKET SKEWERS

Mustard-Thyme Glaze:

   2 tablespoons Dijon-style mustard
   2 tablespoons apricot preserves
   1 teaspoon lemon juice
   1/2 teaspoon dried thyme
   1/4 teaspoon pepper

   1 boneless beef top sirloin steak, cut 1-inch thick
      (about 1-1/4 pounds)
   1 medium yellow squash, sliced (1/2-inch)
   1 medium zucchini, sliced (1/2-inch)
   1 small red onion, cut into 1/2-inch thick
      wedges

8 medium mushrooms
1 tablespoon Dijon-style mustard
1 tablespoon olive oil

Combine glaze ingredients in 1-cup glass measure. Microwave on HIGH 45 seconds, stirring once. Brush on beef steak. Alternately thread vegetables onto four 12-inch metal skewers. Combine mustard and oil; brush on vegetables. Place steak and skewers on grid over medium, ash-covered coals. Grill steak, uncovered, 17 to 21 minutes for medium rare to medium doneness, turning occasionally. Grill vegetables 6 to 10 minutes or until tender, turning occasionally. Carve steak; season with salt. Serve with vegetables. *Makes 4 servings.*

Nutrition Information Per Serving: 308 calories; 36 g protein; 14 g carbohydrate; 12 g fat

GRILLED BEEF EYE ROUND STEAKS WITH GARLIC-YOGURT MARINADE

Marinade & Sauce:
1 cup plain yogurt
1/4 cup chopped fresh parsley
2 tablespoons lemon juice
1 tablespoon sweet paprika
1 tablespoon minced garlic
1 teaspoon salt

1/4 cup mayonnaise
4 beef eye round steaks, cut 1-inch thick (about 8
      ounces each)
Salt

Combine all marinade/sauce ingredients except mayonnaise in small bowl; mix well. Divide mixture in half. Place beef steaks and 1/2 of mixture in food-safe plastic bag; turn steaks to coat. Close bag securely and marinate in refrigerator 6 hours or overnight. Stir mayonnaise into remaining 1/2 of mixture for sauce; cover and refrigerate. Remove steaks from marinade; discard marinade. Place steaks on grid over medium, ash-covered coals. Grill, uncovered, 19 to 23 minutes for medium rare doneness, turning occasionally. (Do not overcook.) Season steaks with salt, as desired. Serve with sauce. *Makes 4 servings.*

Nutrition Information Per Serving, using eye round: calories, 381; carbs, 9

GRILLED T-BONE STEAKS WITH BARBECUE RUB

Barbecue Rub:
   2 tablespoons chili powder
   2 tablespoons packed brown sugar
   1 tablespoon ground cumin

2 teaspoons minced garlic
2 teaspoons cider vinegar
1 teaspoon Worcestershire sauce
1/4 teaspoon ground red pepper

2 to 4 well-trimmed beef T-Bone or porterhouse
    steaks, cut 1-inch thick (about 2 to 4 pounds)
Salt

Combine rub ingredients; press evenly onto beef steaks. Place steaks on grid over medium, ash-covered coals. Grill, uncovered, 14 to 16 minutes for medium rare to medium doneness, turning occasionally. Remove bones and carve steaks into slices, if desired. Season with salt, as desired. *Makes 4 servings.*

Nutrition Information Per Serving, using 2 steaks: calories, 263; carbs, 10

LEMON-HERB BEEF POT ROAST

Seasoning:
2 teaspoons lemon pepper
2 cloves garlic, minced
1 teaspoon dried basil

1 boneless beef chuck pot roast (3 to 3-1/2 pounds)
1 tablespoon olive oil
1 cup water

2 cups baby carrots
1 pound small red-skinned potatoes, halved
1 medium onion, cut into 6 wedges
2 tablespoons cornstarch dissolved in
    2 tablespoons water
1/2 teaspoon dried basil

Combine seasoning ingredients; press onto beef pot roast. Heat oil in Dutch oven over medium heat until hot. Brown pot roast. Pour off drippings. Add 1 cup water; bring to a boil. Reduce heat; cover tightly and simmer 2 hours. Add vegetables; continue cooking, covered, 30 to 45 minutes or until pot roast and vegetables are fork-tender. Remove pot roast and vegetables; keep warm. Skim fat from cooking liquid. Stir in cornstarch mixture and 1/2 teaspoon basil. Cook and stir 1 minute or until thickened and bubbly. Carve pot roast. Serve with vegetables and sauce. *Makes 6 servings.*

Nutrition Information Per Serving: calories, 391; carbs, 21

PEPPER-RUBBED SHOULDER CENTER STEAK

4 beef shoulder center steaks, cut 3/4-inch thick
    (about 5 ounces each)
1 teaspoon cracked black pepper or mixed cracked
    peppercorns (black, white, green and pink)

1 teaspoon minced garlic
2 teaspoons vegetable oil
1/2 cup ready-to-serve beef broth
1/4 cup dry red wine

Combine pepper and garlic; press evenly onto beef steaks. Heat oil in large nonstick skillet over medium heat until hot. Place steaks in skillet; cook 9 to 11 minutes for medium rare to medium doneness, turning once. Remove to platter; keep warm. Add broth and wine to skillet; increase heat to medium-high. Cook and stir 1 to 2 minutes or until browned bits attached to skillet are dissolved and sauce is reduced by half. Spoon sauce over steaks. *Makes 4 servings.*
  Nutrition Information Per Serving: calories, 215; carbs, 1

PEPPERY BEEF TRI-TIP WITH SKEWERED VEGETABLES

Seasoning:
    1 tablespoon packed brown sugar
    2 teaspoons cracked black pepper
    2 cloves garlic, minced
    1/2 teaspoon salt
    1/2 teaspoon dried thyme

    1 beef tri-tip roast (1-1/2 to 2 pounds)
    1/2 cup prepared Italian dressing

6 cups assorted vegetables (onion wedges, 3/4-inch
zucchini or yellow squash slices, 1-inch red bell
pepper pieces, medium mushrooms)

Combine seasoning ingredients. Mix 1 teaspoon with dressing. Press remaining seasoning onto beef roast. Alternately thread vegetables onto 12-inch metal skewers; brush with dressing. Place roast on grid over medium, ash-covered coals. Grill, uncovered, 35 to 45 minutes for medium rare to medium doneness, turning occasionally. Grill vegetables 20 to 25 minutes or until tender, turning occasionally. Remove roast when instant-read thermometer registers 140° F for medium rare; 155° F for medium. Tent loosely with aluminum foil; let stand 10 minutes. (Temperature will continue to rise to 145° F for medium rare; 160° F for medium.) Carve across the grain into thin slices. Serve with vegetables. *Makes 6 to 8 servings.*

Nutrition Information Per Serving: calories, 261; carbs, 10

ASIAN BEEF SALAD

2 boneless beef top loin steaks, cut 1-inch thick
(about 1-1/4 pounds)
1/2 medium red onion, cut into thin wedges
3 tablespoons chopped fresh cilantro
4 cups torn salad greens or sliced Napa cabbage

2 tablespoons chopped peanuts (optional)

Citrus-Soy Dressing:
   2 tablespoons fresh lime juice
   2 tablespoons soy sauce
   1 tablespoon sugar
   2 teaspoons dark sesame oil
   1 serrano pepper, seeded, finely chopped
   1 large clove garlic, minced

Heat large nonstick skillet over medium heat until hot. Place beef steaks in skillet; cook 12 to 15 minutes for medium rare to medium doneness, turning occasionally. Remove; let stand 10 minutes. Whisk dressing ingredients in small bowl until blended. Carve steaks. Combine beef, onion and cilantro in medium bowl. Add dressing; toss. Serve on salad greens. Sprinkle with peanuts. *Makes 4 servings.*

Nutrition Information Per Serving: calories, 275; carbs, 8

MEDITERRANEAN BRAISED BEEF

   1 boneless beef chuck shoulder pot roast (2-1/2
      to 3 pounds)
   1/4 cup all-purpose flour
   2 tablespoons olive oil
   1 1/12 cups water
   1/4 cup balsamic vinegar

2 small onions, halved, sliced
4 medium shallots, sliced
1/4 cup chopped pitted dates
1/2 teaspoon salt
1/4 to 1/2 teaspoon pepper

Heat oven to 325° F. Lightly coat beef pot roast with flour. Heat oil in Dutch oven over medium heat until hot. Brown pot roast; remove. Add 1-1/2 cups water and vinegar to Dutch oven; cook and stir until brown bits attached to pan are dissolved. Return pot roast. Add onions, shallots, dates, salt and pepper; bring to a boil. Cover tightly and cook in 325° F oven 2 to 2-1/2 hours or until pot roast is fork-tender. Remove pot roast; keep warm. Cook liquid and vegetables over medium-high heat to desired consistency. Carve pot roast. Serve with sauce. *Makes 6 to 8 servings.*

Nutrition information per serving: calories, 329; carbs, 16

LAMB

(Recipes courtesy of the American Lamb Board)

Americans eat only 1.3 pounds a year each of lamb. It's a shame because lamb is a meat that is succulent, red, nonfatty and, like all meats, contains no carbs.

ROSEMARY GRILLED LAMB LOIN CHOPS WITH CRANBERRY AND PEPPERED APPLE RELISH

2 tablespoons olive oil
2 tablespoons fresh rosemary leaves, finely chopped
4 double-cut American Lamb loin chops
1 teaspoon salt
4 teaspoons coarse ground black pepper
Cranberry and Peppered Apple Relish (recipe below)

Combine olive oil and rosemary. Dip chops in mixture. Season with salt and pepper. Cover and refrigerate for 1 hour. Grill over medium-hot coals about 20 minutes or to desired degree of doneness: 145° F for medium-rare, 160° F for medium or 170° F for well. Internal temperature will rise approximately 10 degrees. Serve with Cranberry and Peppered Apple Relish. *Makes 4 servings.*

Nutrition Information Per Serving: calories, 299; carbs, 17

CRANBERRY AND PEPPERED APPLE RELISH

1/4 cup dried cranberries
1/4 cup apple juice, heated
1 Granny Smith apple, chopped into 1/2-inch pieces
1/4 cup fresh or frozen cranberries

1 tablespoon olive oil
1 tablespoon balsamic vinegar
1 teaspoon course ground black pepper
1 teaspoon brown sugar, packed
pinch salt

Combine all ingredients.

Tip: This relish is best made a day ahead to allow flavors to blend.

CELEBRATION LEG OF LAMB

1 tablespoon soy sauce
1 tablespoon olive oil
1 clove garlic, crushed
1 teaspoon pepper
1/2 teaspoon ground ginger
1 whole bay leaf, crushed
1/2 teaspoon dried thyme
1/2 teaspoon dried sage
1/2 teaspoon dried marjoram
6 to 9 pounds American Lamb leg, bone-in

In small bowl, mix together soy sauce, olive oil, garlic, pepper, ginger, bay leaf, thyme, sage and marjoram. Place lamb on rack in roasting pan. With sharp knife, make frequent slits in surface of lamb. Move knife from side to side to enlarge pockets. Rub herb mixture into each slit. Rub any remaining mixture over roast. Roast in 325° F oven for 20 to 25 minutes per pound or until meat thermometer registers 145° F for medium-rare, 160° F for medium or 170° F for well. Remove roast from oven, cover and let stand 10 minutes. Internal temperature will rise approximately 10 degrees. Pan drippings can be used in gravy or skimmed and served au jus. *Makes 12 servings.*

Nutrition Information Per Serving: calories, 382; carbs, .37

SEAFOOD

(Recipes courtesy of www.shrimp.com)

GARLIC SKEWERED SHRIMP

  1 1/2 pounds jumbo shrimp
  1/2 cup canola oil
  2 cloves garlic
  2 tablespoons red wine vinegar
  1 tablespoon chopped fresh basil
  Salt and pepper to taste

Shell and devein shrimp. Mix other ingredients. Toss with shrimp and refrigerate 1 hour or more, tossing occasionally. Remove shrimp, reserving marinade. Bend each shrimp almost in half and insert skewer so it passes through shrimp twice. Grill about 8 minutes, or until cooked through, turning frequently and brushing at least twice with marinade. *Makes 4 appetizer servings.*

Nutrition Information Per Serving: calories, 180; carbs, 0

BROCCOLI AND MUSHROOM SCALLOPS

1 1/2 pounds jumbo scallops
2 cups sliced mushrooms
2 tablespoons margarine or butter
3 cups cut broccoli
2 ounces sliced pimientos
1 can condensed chicken broth
3 tablespoons cornstarch
2 teaspoons lite soy sauce

Cut scallops into halves. In a 3-quart saucepan, cook and stir mushrooms in margarine or butter over medium heat until tender. Stir in scallops, broccoli and pimientos. Cook, stirring frequently, until scallops are white and firm (about 3 to 4 minutes). Gradually stir chicken broth into cornstarch until smooth. Stir broth mixture and soy sauce into scallop mixture. Heat to boiling, stirring constantly. Reduce heat, simmer and stir 1 minute. Serve

over low-carb pasta. *Makes 4 servings.*
Nutrition Information Per Serving: Calories, 160; carbs, 22

SHRIMP SCAMPI

2 pounds large shrimp, pre-cooked, shelled, deveined, with tails on
1/2 pound butter, melted
1 lemon, sliced
1 teaspoon Dijon mustard
2 tablespoons chopped parsley
1 teaspoon Worcestershire sauce*
4 cloves garlic, pressed
1/2 teaspoon chili powder*
1/2 teaspoon paprika*
salt and pepper to taste
Reduce these ingredients for a less-tangy dish

Combine all ingredients, except shrimp, and set aside. Place shrimp on flat baking pan. Pour sauce over shrimp and refrigerate for 24 hours. When ready to serve, bake for 20 minutes at 350° F, basting often. Place under broiler for 1 to 2 minutes, until shrimp tails turn brown. *Makes 6 servings.*
Nutrition Information Per Serving: calories, 180; carbs, 0

BAKED OYSTERS APPETIZER

24 large oysters
1/2 cup low-carb flour
1 teaspoon salt
1/8 teaspoon pepper
2 large eggs, slightly beaten
1/2 cup butter, melted
6 lemon wedges

Heat oven to 425° F. Grease shallow baking pan with butter. Mix flour, salt and pepper. Drain oysters, dry with paper towels and roll in the flour mixture. Then dip them in the egg and roll in flour again. Arrange oysters in baking pan. Pour melted butter over each. Bake 10 to 15 minutes, or until oysters are slightly browned, basting twice. Garnish with lemon wedges. *Serves 4.*

Nutrition Information Per Serving: calories, 118; carbs, 24

TUNA SALAD AND SHRIMP

1 pound large shrimp, precooked
2 cans white tuna in water
1 small can salmon
3 tablespoons mayonnaise
8-ounce jar sweet relish
3 large eggs
1 white onion

1 small bell pepper
salt and pepper, or commercial seasoning, to taste

Hard boil eggs. Mix tuna and salmon with mayo. Chop onion, slice peppers and add to relish, chopped eggs and season. Then add shrimp and chill for at least two hours. *Serves 6.*

Nutrition Information Per Serving: calories, 180; carbs 11

SHRIMP EGG FOO YUNG

4 large eggs
1 pound large shrimp, peeled, deveined and cooked
4 tablespoons peanut oil
1/4 cup chopped onion
1/4 cup chopped mushroom
1 large scallion, chopped
1 cup fresh bean sprouts
1/2 teaspoon sugar

Sauce:
2 teaspoons cornstarch
1/2 cup chicken broth
1 tablespoon lite soy sauce
1/4 teaspoon ground ginger
1/2 teaspoon dry mustard

Beat eggs until light. Cut shrimp into small

pieces. Saute onions, mushrooms and scallion in 1 tablespoon of peanut oil for 1 minute. Then add bean sprouts and shrimp and toss. Add soy sauce and sugar, mixing well. Place in large bowl and add eggs. In a wide skillet, heat remaining oil and ladle in 1/4 of egg mixture to make one omelet. Cook until eggs are brown on one side. Then turn and brown the other. Repeat until four omelets are cooked.

Sauce: Stir cornstarch into chicken broth to dissolve. Add soy sauce, ginger and mustard. Bring to a boil, cook until mixture thickens. Pour over omelet.

Serve with stir-fried fresh vegetables — pre-cooked cauliflower, snow peas, scallions, bok choy — chopped or sliced. Put two table- spoons peanut oil, 1/4 teaspoon ground ginger, 1 tablespoon lite soy sauce and 1/2 crushed gar- lic clove into saute pan and cook vegetables over 375° F heat, stirring rapidly and continu- ously until tender. *Makes 2 servings.*

Nutrition Information Per Serving: calories, 450; carbs, 7

OYSTER SALAD

 24 large oysters
 2 large tomatoes, sliced thin
 6 teaspoons lemon juice
 1 cup diced celery

12 leaves of red leaf lettuce
Mayonnaise
Paprika

Place oysters, in the half shell, in baking pan and bake in their own juice at 325° F until the edges curl up. Drain and chill. Place a lettuce leaf on each of four salad plates. Shred the rest if the lettuce and place on lettuce leaves. Lay 6 oysters on each and sprinkle with lemon juice. Carefully twist tomato slices, placing 2 or 3 on each plate. Add celery. Dab oysters with mayonnaise, sprinkle with paprika and chill for 1 hour before serving. *Make 4 servings.*

Nutrition Information Per Serving: calories, 123; carbs, 4

SHRIMP SALAD – SOUTHERN STYLE

1 1/2 pounds large shrimp, peeled, deveined and
    chopped
Old Bay Seasoning
1/2 cup finely diced celery
1/2 cup finely diced cucumber
2 tablespoons minced shallots or yellow onion
1/2 cup mayonnaise
2 tablespoons lemon juice
salt and pepper to taste

Boil the shrimp in Old Bay Seasoning or your

own favorite commercial brand the day before and refrigerate so the shrimp will become well-seasoned. Combine all ingredients and refrigerate until cold. Serve on a bed of romaine lettuce.

Nutrition Information Per Serving: calories, 241; carbs, 1

The recipes in this chapter are only a few of the scrumptious dishes available on the Web sites of the contributing organizations. You'll find those Internet addresses in our resources chapter later in this book.

FAVORITES

Here are a few of my personal favorites from the Barnhill family kitchen. All of them are under 300 calories and 15 grams of carbohydrates per serving.

SEAFOOD STEW

1 1/2 pounds white fish (flounder, cod, halibut)
2 green peppers
2 large onions
2 large tomatoes
8 large mushrooms
1 can peeled tomatoes, with juice
1 small can (single serving) tomato juice

3 cloves crushed garlic
1 tablespoon anise seed
1/2 teaspoon ground thyme
salt and pepper to taste
2 tablespoons olive oil
1 teaspoon sugar

Slice onions, peppers and mushrooms and saute in olive oil until tender, stirring often. Set aside. Wash fish and gently pat dry. Crush canned tomatoes and place in large saute pan with garlic, anise seed, thyme, sugar, salt and pepper. Heat over high heat until boiling and add tomato juice. When mixture comes to boil again, lower heat and gently place fish into pan, making sure it is covered with hot juices, and add vegetables. Cook for 3 to 5 minutes, or until fish is white and firm. *Makes 4 servings.*

Nutrition Information Per Serving (approx): calories, 240; carbs, 12

SEA AND FARM MEDLEY

1 1/2 pound firm fish (yellowfin tuna, swordfish, Chilean sea bass)
1 large green pepper, halved
1 large onion, pre-boiled
1 medium zucchini, sliced length-wise, skin on
6 large mushrooms

1/2 pound pre-boiled fresh cauliflower
2 large ripe tomatoes, halved
1/4 cup olive oil
1 tablespoon red wine vinegar
3 cloves crushed garlic
salt and pepper to taste

Mix olive oil, garlic, salt and pepper to make sauce. Brush sauce over vegetables and place all but tomatoes about 6 inches above hot coals on grill. Watch carefully, turning once, until vegetables BEGIN getting tender. Then add tomatoes and fish. Cook until fish is white and firm, brushing with sauce occasionally. *Makes 4 servings*.

Tip: Place a fish grill with very small openings over your main grill to prevent tender pieces from falling into hot coals.

Nutrition Information Per Serving: calories, 280; carbs 13

PINEAPPLE GRILLED SALMON

Marinade:
1/2 cup unsweetened pineapple juice
1/4 cup lemon juice
1/4 cup olive oil
1 teaspoon dill
salt and pepper to taste

4 thick salmon steaks

Combine ingredients to create a marinade in a large bowl. Add salmon steaks, making sure they are coated. Cover tightly and refrigerate for 2 hours, shaking occasionally to re-coat salmon. Measure thickness of salmon. Then place steaks on grill about six inches over hot coals. Cook 10 minutes for each inch of thickness, turning at the halfway point and basting with the leftover marinade. Serve with lemon-wedge garnish. *Makes 4 servings.*

Nutrition Information Per Serving: calories, 314; carbs, 9.

CHICKEN SCALLOPINI

2 boneless chicken breasts, skin removed
2 tablespoons butter
2 tablespoons flour
1 cup chicken broth
2 lemon wedges

Carefully slice breasts horizontally into 1/2-inch slabs and flatten between rolling pin and cutting board. Dip chicken slabs into flour. Melt butter in saute pan and brown chicken on both sides at medium heat. Set aside and keep warm in oven. Pour chicken broth into saute pan, increase heat and reduce to thicken. Place chicken into serving tray and cover with sauce. Garnish with lemon quarters. Serve with low-carb pasta. *Makes 2 servings.*

CHICKEN PROVENCAL

2 split chicken breasts and 4 thighs, skin
    removed
1/2 cup olive oil
1 cup dry white wine
2 cloves crushed garlic
1 can peeled tomatoes, crushed
1/3 cup lean ham, sliced thin and chopped
1/2 teaspoon thyme
1/2 teaspoon oregano
1/2 teaspoon basil
1 cup mixed green and black olives, sliced
salt and pepper to taste

Heat olive oil in large saute pan and cook chicken until brown on both sides. Add tomatoes, ham, wine and seasonings and simmer over low heat for 20 to 30 minutes, stirring and turning chicken. Then add olives and cook 3-5 minutes longer. Place chicken in serving dish and set aside. Increase heat under sauce and cook 5 minutes to reduce. Then pour over chicken.

SHISH KEBAB

Marinade:
- 2 tablespoons red wine vinegar
- 2 tablespoons lemon juice
- 1/2 to 3/4 cup olive oil
- 1/4 teaspoon ground cumin
- 1/2 teaspoon crumbled rosemary
- 2 cloves crushed garlic
- 1/4 teaspoon thyme
- salt and pepper to taste

- 1 pound lamb or steak, in large chunks
- 2 large tomatoes
- 1 large green pepper
- 1 large yellow onion
- 4 large mushrooms

Marinade: Mix 2 tablespoons red wine vinegar, 2 tablespoons lemon juice, 1/2 to 3/4 cup olive oil, 1/4 teaspoon ground cumin, 1/2 teaspoon crumbled rosemary, two cloves crushed garlic, 1/4 teaspoon thyme, salt and pepper to taste. Mix well.

Place cubed lamb and marinade in covered dish and refrigerate overnight. Halve tomatoes and green pepper. Pre-boil onion until slightly tender. Remove lamb from marinade and brush marinade over vegetables. Place vegetables

about six inches over hot coals and cook until
tender, basting occasionally. Remove to metal
tray and place at edge of grill to keep warm, but
not cook. Then place cubed lamb on grill and
cook 3 to 5 minutes, basting occasionally.
Remove lamb while still pink in center. *Makes 2
servings.*

GRILLED OR BROILED STEAK – A TRADITIONAL AMERICAN TREAT

1 teaspoon olive oil
1 crushed garlic clove
1 pound lean beef – sirloin, T-bone, chuck eye –
   cut at least 1-inch thick

Mix oil and garlic and brush onto both sides
of steak. Place about 6 inches above gray ash-
covered coals on grill for 5 minutes on each side
for medium rare. Serve with choice of green
vegetables or mashed boiled cauliflower with a
pat of butter on top. *Makes 2 servings.*

ENRICHED HAMBURGER WITH FARM-FRESH GRILLED VEGETABLES

1 pound lean ground chuck
1/2 medium onion
1 large egg

1 small zucchini
2 large mushrooms
1 green bell pepper
4 cauliflower florets
3 tablespoon olive oil
1/8 teaspoon salt
1 clove garlic

Chop onion finely. Combine onion and egg with ground chuck and mix well. Gently form into 2 to 4 patties. Combine crushed garlic glove, salt and olive oil and brush onto vegetables. Place vegetables and beef patties about 6 inches from gray ash-covered coals on grill for 10 minutes, turning as needed. *Makes 2 servings.*

CHINESE BEEF AND VEGETABLES

1 1/2 pound chuck roast, sliced thin
1 large onion
1 large bell pepper
4 large cauliflower florets
2 teaspoons lite soy sauce
1/2 teaspoon oyster sauce
1/4 teaspoon ground ginger
3 tablespoons peanut oil
1/2 cup brown rice
1/4 teaspoon salt

In boiling water, pre-cook cauliflower until slightly soft and set aside. Stir rice and salt into 1 cup boiling water. Cover tightly and cook 20 minutes on lowest heat setting possible. Meanwhile, cut onion in half and slice. Core pepper and slice into strips. Cook pepper and onion in peanut oil over high heat, stirring rapidly, until they begin losing crispness. Then lower heat to medium and add cauliflower, beef, soy sauce, oyster sauce and ginger. Stir rapidly until beads of blood appear on beef. Remove and serve over rice. *Makes 4 servings.*

GRILLED PORK CHOPS WITH CHEESE AND GARLIC CAULIFLOWER

  2 large center-cut pork chops, cut at least 1-inch
    thick
  1/2 small cauliflower
  1/4 cup milk
  4-6 ounces very sharp Cheddar cheese
  2 cloves crushed garlic
  3 tablespoons teriyaki sauce
  4 ounces unsalted butter
  salt and pepper to taste

This is a meal best made by two. Boil cauliflower until tender and set aside. Cut cheese into very small cubes, or shred. Melt butter in small saute pan and when hot, slowly add cheese, stirring continuously, then add crushed garlic. Place cauliflower in large bowl, add milk, and beat with mixer until fully whipped. Then pour in cheese sauce and beat until well mixed. Meanwhile, the assistant cook should brush teriyaki sauce over chops and place about six inches over hot coals. Watch carefully, turning and basting often, until meat is firm, and cooked through. *Makes 2 servings.*

CHAPTER 10

TURNING BACK SNACK ATTACKS

OK, but what about snacks? Americans are the world's champion snackers, quaffing billions of pounds of munchables every year, most of it in front of their TV sets at night. And you can prove it by our waistlines.

According to the American Snack Food Association, Americans consume a staggering $6 billion-plus a year in munchable snacks — potato chips, tortilla chips, pretzels, popcorn and pork rinds among the most popular — 22.61 pounds a year for every man, woman and child in the United States.

But a lot of nighttime snacking is out of habit; a form of entertainment and stress relief. Americans watch a lot of TV, a sedentary form of entertainment that many people associate with snacking. So when the TV goes on, the hand goes into the snack bowl. If you ask snackers if they're really hungry, the answer often is not really — but still they snack. For some, the amount of snacking that goes on from dinnertime until Jay Leno can be the equivalent of another meal.

Some people eat from boredom, others eat under stress and when they're anxious or excited. Emotions and eating, unfortunately, often go together. People release their emotions in the kitchen rather than nonfood outlets.

We all have stress and we need to find a healthy mechanism to manage it. Some of us go for walks, some call a friend, some take a hot bubble bath — and some go to the kitchen for a snack. We all have these emotions, it's how we handle them that's the difference. Unfortunately when you manage your stress with food, it could, literally, feed in to a weight problem.

Obviously, if you avoid those snacks and do something else, you can cut a lot of extra calories from your diet. And if you do that every night, it can be an easy way to trim some unwanted pounds.

Not all snacks are created equal. Stick to low-carb items and don't overdo them. Check pages 76-77 for some great low-carb, low-fat snacks. Plus, here are a few tips that will help you cut back on evening snacks:

1. Fall out of love with your TV. Television is filled with appetite-triggers, ads touting a variety of tasty foods that can stimulate your taste buds and make a trip to the fridge a must. So divorcing your TV set could help you cut back on snack attacks.

2. When a snack attack comes on, drown it. A tall glass of water or sugarless decaf iced tea often can quell the desire for a nighttime snack. Not only will it make you feel full, but it will satisfy the need to put something in your mouth.

3. Brush away desire. When you feel the urge for a snack, brush your teeth and floss. The activity will satisfy the hands-to-mouth urge and the taste of the toothpaste will give the illusion you've eaten something sweet.

4. Sweet surrender. When the urge to splurge comes on, try a piece of really good sugarless candy or a fat-free pudding desert. A couple of handfuls of air-popped popcorn (with no butter on it) also can fill the bill.

5. Tutty-fruittie. If you really feel the need, gobble down a fresh orange, apple or some other kind of fruit instead of ice cream, candy or potato chips. The fruit will fill, without empty calories.

6. Rate your snack attack — and give it a 0. Most people never think about nighttime snacks; one minute they're in front of the TV and the next they're in the kitchen eating something they'll later wish they hadn't. Before heading to the fridge, think about your urge and give it a score. Are you really hungry? Do you need the calories for energy just an hour or two before bed? If the score comes up 0, head back to the TV — empty-handed.

7. Don't fill idle hands with food. Grandma used to say "idle hands are the devil's workshop." But she might have said idle hands are a sign of boredom and sometimes we alleviate boredom with food. So, get busy when you feel a snack attack coming on. Go for a short, brisk walk, play with the kids or your pet, start a crossword puzzle, do your nails, anything that gets your hands in motion — without food in them.

8. Plan ahead. Most of us fill the snack urge with the first appealing thing that comes to hand, no matter how fattening or unhealthy. So prepare ahead for your snack attack by stocking up on healthy, nutritious, non-fattening snacks — fresh fruit and low-carb desserts.

9. Take flight. Get as far away from the fridge as you can, even if it means leaving the house for a while. The more effort it takes to go to the kitchen and get a snack, the less likely you are to do it. And if you can put off the craving for just a few minutes, get your mind off it, the urge could pass. If you're going to watch TV or read, do it in the bedroom.

10. Count to 10. When you feel the urge to splurge, take a relaxation break; stretch out, close your eyes and count to 10 while you conjure up a pleasant, relaxing image until the need to feed passes.

11. Open a "snackable bank account." There's no law against nighttime snacking; it's what you eat that's important, not when, experts say. A delicious piece of chocolate is as fattening at night as it is after lunch. So plan for your snack attacks by saving some calories during your daytime eating — if you put 100 calories into the bank at lunch and dinner, you can spend them in the evening.

12. Put temptation behind you — leave it in the supermarket. Don't buy the foods that tempt you. Erase ice cream, potato chips and cookies from your shopping list. That way when you get the urge, they won't be there, and if you really want them, you'll have to drive to the supermarket. That can take a real bite out of your appetite for a snack.

Is your snacking just a way to fend off boredom, relieve stress or tickle your sweet tooth — or is it a sign of night-eating syndrome?

Night-eating syndrome — snack attacks to the extreme — recently was recognized by the medical profession as an eating disorder in which the symptom is not only snacking after dinner, but actually waking during the night with an uncontrollable urge to chow down.

In a study published in the *Journal of the American Medical Association*, University of Pennsylvania psychiatrist Albert Stunkard, M.D., reported that people with night-eating syndrome have little appetite during the day, but consume a whopping 56 percent of their calories between 8 p.m. and 6 a.m. He estimated 1.5 percent of Americans suffer the syndrome.

Nighttime snacking can cause more problems than weight gain. Dr. Stunkard reports the 10 people he studied who ate carbohydrate-rich snacks at night woke from sleep 178 times a week, compared to only 13 times for those who didn't snack. Moreover, the heavy snackers suffered mood swings during the day.

So if you're rarely very hungry during the day but often wake up starving at night, talk to your doctor; you may have a treatable problem.

And next time you crave a tasty tidbit, go back to Chapter 8 and pick tasty — and non-fattening — snacks suggested by Barry Sears for his Zone Diet.

CHAPTER 11

AWAY FROM HOME

Government surveys show Americans, on average, eat at least one meal a day away from home. And every one of those meals is an opportunity to pack on pounds.

To cater to bargain-hungry Americans, restaurants, especially the fast-food chains, have developed the super-size concept; for just a few pennies more, you get a giant-size order of food.

Don't swallow that! These portions are far more than you need. So pocket those extra pennies and leave the extra calories in the kitchen. Your waistline will love you for it.

It really won't be all that hard because more and more restaurants are leaping aboard the low-carb bandwagon. And that's good news for you.

Many now have special low-carb menus, or

designate low-carb offerings in their main menu. Subway offers Atkins-approved subs and salads. Burger King offers a bunless burger and McDonald's not only offers "Go Active" choices for dieters, but it also gives you a pedometer with them to encourage you to move more.

Even restaurants that don't offer special low-carb menu choices are willing to prepare special dishes to order. And, of course, you can always ask that the high-carb, high-fat items be left in the kitchen.

Chili's boasts an "It's Your Choice" menu with 14 low-carb dishes. Ruby Tuesday lets you choose from 40 low-carb dishes and provides detailed nutritional information for each. T.G.I. Friday's offers Atkins-approved foods and provides net carb counts for each.

The low-carb conscious restaurant list goes on and on, as the low-carb movement continues to grow. But there's a bottom line (no pun intended): The final responsibility is yours. When you dine out, think Ultimate — would this dish fit into my Ultimate Low-Carb Plan?

Here are a few helpful hints nutritional experts say will let you leave the calories behind when you dine out:

● Ask your server for nutrition information (for example, calories, saturated fat and sodium) before you order.

● Choose foods that are steamed, broiled, baked, roasted, poached or stir-fried, but not deep-fat fried.

● Share food, such as a main dish or dessert, with your dining partner.

● Take part of the food home with you and refrigerate immediately. You may want to ask for a take-home container when the meal arrives. Spoon half the meal into it, so you're likely to eat only what's left on your plate.

● Request your meal to be served without gravy, sauces, butter or margarine. Ask for salad dressing on the side and use only small amounts of full-fat dressings.

● Ask your server to give you fat-free (skim) milk rather than whole milk or cream and to trim visible fat from poultry or meat. Ask that the chef use less oil when cooking your meal.

● Finally, buy a small carb counter (one that counts fats, as well, would be even better) and carry it with you when you eat outside your home. It'll let you go over the menu and, lightening-fast, calculate the carb and fat levels in each dish.

And a word of advice for the holidays:

Studies show many Americans pick up a pound or more between Thanksgiving and New Year's Day. Traditionally, it's a time people throw caution to the wind and pig out. Bad choice! Especially since it's perfectly possible to pig out on low-carb choices without packing on pounds.

So here are some words of wisdom:

● **Don't even think about losing during that month-plus**; instead, focus on maintaining your current weight.

● **Make careful choices** when the buffet table at a party is groaning under the dozens of tasty tidbits — take very small tastes of the more healthful offerings and try to stay away from the high-carb, high-fat dishes.

CHAPTER 12

MOVING YOUR FAT AWAY

We've talked about dining at home, snacking and eating out. Now it's time to tackle another major barrier to weight loss: lack of exercise.

Only 45 percent of Americans now get regular exercise at least five days a week. The rest of us have become couch potatoes. And no diet in the world, short of having yourself sealed in a barrel, will help you lose weight and keep it off if you don't get moving.

When you cut back on carbs, fats and calories without exercise, your weight loss will be 75 percent fat — and 25 percent good, lean body mass, the weight you don't want to lose. But if you combine activity and dieting, the loss will be a whopping 98 percent fat. That's impressive! And irrefutable proof physical movement should be an important part of your new Ultimate lifestyle.

Health experts recommend at least 30 minutes a day of physical activity, even if it's nothing more than taking the stairs at work, parking your car a few blocks from your destination or playing a little more with the kids.

Activity increases the rate at which your body metabolizes fats and even a 30-minute moderate workout can hike your metabolic rate by 10 percent — and keep it up for six to 24 hours — and for some people, as much as 48 hours. That's a whole lot of benefit for very little effort.

Oh, and before I forget, when you get yourself moving, the benefits won't only be in the loss of fat; exercise can help you ward off things like heart disease, osteoporosis, high blood pressure, arthritis and even some forms of cancer. Even a short workout can actually decrease your hunger, studies show.

If you aren't active now, start slooooooooowly. Walk just five minutes a day the first week. Then jump it to eight minutes for as long as it takes for you to feel really comfortable at this level. Then you can increase your walks to 11 minutes and slowly add another four minutes, one at a time. By the time you're comfortable at this level, you'll be ready to kick your speed up.

A few suggestions from some of the nation's leading fitness experts:

● **Keep an activity log** to track your progress. Jot down the days and times you exercised, what you did and for how long. Make a private note: How did the workout make you feel?

● **Be comfortable** during your workout. Dress appropriately. Wear comfortable walking shoes with a lot of support and clothes that don't chafe your inner thighs as you walk — spandex shorts, or tights, for example.

● **Enlist support.** Try to get your partner, children or a friend to join you in your workouts. Try a long walk with your partner. Play with the kids in the afternoon. Or you might enroll in a dance class with friends. Anything that provides pleasant company during your workouts.

● **Take two- or three-minute walking breaks** at work every day.

● **Get rid of the remote.** One recent study showed just getting up and down to change the TV channels can burn off two pounds during the course of a year. Who would have thought it?

Here's how many calories you can scorch in a single hour of movement:

❏ Ballroom dancing will burn off 326 calories, for you AND your partner.

❏ A bike ride will consume 470 calories.

❑ Cleaning house, 259
❑ Dusting, 169
❑ Gardening, 345
❑ Shopping for groceries, 259
❑ Doing laundry, 153
❑ Mowing the lawn, 345
❑ Raking the lawn, 364
❑ Making dinner, 157

Some exercise calorie counts are surprising, even humorous. For example, did you know if you brush your teeth for five minutes, as your dentist suggests, you'll burn off 15 calories a day? And making the bed will burn another 12.

Sleeping burns 60 an hour and eating burns 70 calories every 30 minutes, so long, leisurely dinners might be just what the doctor ordered.

Reading and watching TV both burn 75 calories an hour. Standing in line burns 100, but chasing the kids only burns off 120. Hmmmmmm. Most moms might think it was A LOT more.

And here's pleasant news: Sexual intimacy will get rid of 108 calories an hour.

Some activities burn more than others. Climbing up and down stairs, for example, will get rid of 425 calories an hour. But you're not likely to do it for an entire hour, so how about climbing the stairs at work, in the mall, or anywhere for three to four minutes at a time. Not a lot of calories to be sure, but over time, they'll add up.

Try to find physical activities you can fit into your daily routine until they become SO routine you don't even think about them. If you think about it, burning off an extra 3,500 calories a week is as easy as eating a slice of low-carb pie. And it will get rid of a pound of fat a week, without even dieting.

Mowing the lawn, instead of hiring a neighborhood kid; doing a whole-house cleaning more often than a few times a year. Washing windows, or the car. A brisk walk or a fast game of softball with the kids. An hour in the garden, perhaps growing your own healthy vegetables. All these will burn off fat.

If you're a large person, you may worry about exercise — will you look funny, awkward, ungainly? Will people laugh at you? Well, here's a flash: Other people are too worried about looking funny, awkward or ungainly to think much about you. We're all in it together. So put away your feelings of self-consciousness and get moving. Now.

Not only will regular physical activity help you shed pounds, but it'll also keep you healthier, helping you ward off a number of serious conditions (like heart disease). It will also relieve stress, improve your moods, help build healthy bones, muscles and joints, improve your self-image and much, much more. You can't lose by moving.

Start slowly. Give yourself time to get used to more physical activity. Add little bits and pieces to your regular daily routine, like climbing the stairs instead of riding the elevator.

If you decide to exercise vigorously, pick something that's fun. Bowling, perhaps; millions do it. Or golf; millions more. Tennis. Racquetball. A pick-up game of basketball at the local playground. Physical activity doesn't have to be a chore. And it sure needn't be a bore.

Give yourself credit for trying, whether you succeed — at first — or not. Keep trying. It'll get easier as you go. And when you begin seeing the result in your mirror, give yourself a pat on the back. You'll have earned it.

Don't rush it. Don't push it. Muscles that haven't been used much for a while will take time to become supple. If you go at it hard, expect some aches and pains. That's what aspirin is for. But if the pain is sharp, intense, in your chest or running down your left arm, it might be a warning. Stop what you're doing and call your doctor.

Set goals. This week, I'll add enough physical activities to burn off X calories. Keep score in your diary. Add up the NEW things you'll do and tote up the calories you'll burn.

Get a loved one or close friend to work with you. People exercise better when they have company.

It's more fun. And your exercise partner can cheer you on.

A note of caution if you have any health conditions — diabetes, heart disease, asthma, arthritis, high blood pressure — talk over your new movement plans with your doctor before beginning.

And for busy homemakers here as some simple aerobic exercises you can do right in your own kitchen:

● **The Knife Edge.** Place both hands on your countertop, then push away, stretching your arms as far as you can. Bend, so your torso is parallel to the floor and alternate standing on each leg for 15 seconds.

● **The Chair Twister.** Sit sideways in a kitchen chair with your hands on the chair's back. Turn and stretch right, then left, holding each for 15 seconds.

● **The Level Choice.** Place two items of equal weight, one in each hand, then stand for 15 seconds on each leg.

● **The Fridge Chiller.** Lean your backside against the fridge, then bend slowly from the waist and hold that position for 10 to 15 seconds before standing upright. Repeat twice.

Many working women just don't have the time for a regular exercise program, between their jobs, caring for the house, cooking meals and looking after children, experts say. So they have to find ways to fit exercise into their daily living routines. This simple kitchen workout can fit right in.

Want something a little tougher? Something that will get rid of pounds AND build some muscle? OK, forget about fancy gyms and expensive equipment; you can get into great shape right in your home and it won't cost you a dime. All you need are a pillow, a small rug and two standard-size cans of soup, says veteran trainer and coach, Doug Brolus.

He calls the workout "Circuit Training", a series of exercise sets done in rapid succession, with only as much rest as an individual needs between them. Brolus, who has worked with Arnold Schwarzenegger and Jack LaLanne, says the workout can be tailored to fit each individual's needs.

As with all strenuous exercise programs, start slowly, doing just a few sets at a time and resting between them as much as you need. As you build strength and endurance, you'll be able to increase the number of sets and lower your resting time between each. Try these, for starters:

● **Squats.** Standing with your legs comfortably spread to shoulder width, toes pointing forward, slowly lower yourself into a sitting position, hold it for one second, then stand.

● **Curls.** Hold a one or two liter bottle in each hand; it's cheaper than buying weights. Stand with your hands at your sides, palms facing forward. Raise your forearms and bend elbows until the cans almost touch your shoulders.

● **Side lateral raises.** Using the same two food cans, palms facing forward, slowly raise your arms straight out from your sides, elbows locked, until the cans are level with your shoulders.

● **Leg lifts.** Lie on your back with your hands behind your head, legs straight. Slowly raise both legs until your heels are about five inches off the ground. Hold for a second, then lower them. You can make this one more difficult by tying an old sock filled with sand around each ankle.

● **Abdominal crunches.** Lie on the back, legs resting on a pillow, hands behind your head. Do a half sit-up, raising your shoulders about five inches over the floor, then lower.

Start out by doing these exercises four to five times each, five days a week, and slowly increase the number of sets, as you are able. Not only will they burn calories and build muscles; they're also good for heart health, Brolus says.

I could go on for dozens of pages, but I'm sure you're getting the idea; a little movement, a lot of fun and pretty soon you have a smaller waistline.

If you look just a little, you'll soon see you have hundreds of opportunities to get yourself moving every day. Walking the dog, for instance; mowing the lawn and raking it afterward, tending the garden — or putting one in, if you don't have one.

CHAPTER 13

COUNTING C's

Here's a handy carb counter to help you follow the low-carb path, provided by experts at the Food and Nutrition Service of the U.S. Department of Agriculture. The following pages contain only a sampling of the thousands of food items in the marketplace, but even more information is at your fingertips.

Go online and type in www.nal.usda.gov/fnic. When the USDA screen opens, click on the "Food Composition" button on the left side of the screen. That will take you to the Food and Nutrition Service's extensive data base of nutrients. Then, just follow the simple directions.

There are other carb counters online. Try www.carb-counter.org, which lists, literally, thousands of foods.

Description

Alcoholic beverage, beer, light

Alcoholic beverage, beer, regular

Alcoholic beverage, daiquiri, prepared-from-recipe

Alcoholic beverage, distilled, all (gin, rum, vodka, whiskey) 80 proof

Alcoholic beverage, distilled, all (gin, rum, vodka, whiskey) 86 proof

Alcoholic beverage, distilled, all (gin, rum, vodka, whiskey) 90 proof

Alcoholic beverage, liqueur, coffee, 53 proof

Alcoholic beverage, pina colada, prepared-from-recipe

Alcoholic beverage, wine, dessert, dry

Alcoholic beverage, wine, dessert, sweet

Alcoholic beverage, wine, table, red

Alcoholic beverage, wine, table, white

Alfalfa seeds, sprouted, raw

Apple juice, canned or bottled, unsweetened, without added ascorbic acid

Apples, dried, sulfured, uncooked

Apples, raw, with skin

Apples, raw, without skin

Applesauce, canned, sweetened, without salt

Applesauce, canned, unsweetened, without added ascorbic acid

Apricot nectar, canned, with added ascorbic acid

Apricots, canned, heavy syrup pack, with skin, solids and liquids

Apricots, canned, juice pack, with skin, solids and liquids

Apricots, dried, sulfured, uncooked

Common Measure	Content per Measure
12 fl oz	4.602
12 fl oz	13.135
2 fl oz	4.164
1.5 fl oz	0.000
1.5 fl oz	0.042
1.5 fl oz	0.000
1.5 fl oz	24.336
4.5 fl oz	31.951
3.5 fl oz	12.020
3.5 fl oz	14.101
3.5 fl oz	1.751
3.5 fl oz	0.824
1 cup	1.247
1 cup	28.966
5 rings	21.085
1 apple	19.058
1 cup	14.036
1 cup	50.771
1 cup	27.548
1 cup	36.119
1 cup	55.393
1 cup	30.110
10 halves	21.924

Description

Apricots, raw

Artichokes, (globe or french), cooked, boiled, drained, without salt

Artichokes, (globe or french), cooked, boiled, drained, without salt

Asparagus, canned, drained solids

Asparagus, cooked, boiled, drained

Asparagus, frozen, cooked, boiled, drained, without salt

Asparagus, frozen, cooked, boiled, drained, without salt

Avocados, raw, California

Avocados, raw, Florida

Bagels, cinnamon-raisin

Bagels, cinnamon-raisin

Bagels, egg

Bagels, egg

Bagels, plain, enriched, with calcium propionate (includes onion, poppy, sesame)

Bagels, plain, enriched, with calcium propionate (includes onion, poppy, sesame)

Baking chocolate, unsweetened, liquid

Baking chocolate, unsweetened, squares

Bamboo shoots, canned, drained solids

Bananas, raw

Bananas, raw

Barley, pearled, cooked

Barley, pearled, raw

Common Measure	Content per Measure
1 apricot	3.892
1 cup	18.782
1 medium	13.416
4 spears	1.771
4 spears	2.466
1 cup	3.456
4 spears	1.152
1 oz	2.449
1 oz	2.217
3-1/2" bagel	39.192
4" bagel	49.128
4" bagel	47.170
3-1/2" bagel	37.630
3-1/2" bagel	37.914
4" bagel	47.526
1 oz	9.611
1 square	8.460
1 cup	4.218
1 banana	26.951
1 cup	34.260
1 cup	44.305
1 cup	155.440

Description

Beans, baked, canned, plain or vegetarian

Beans, baked, canned, with franks

Beans, baked, canned, with pork and sweet sauce

Beans, baked, canned, with pork and tomato sauce

Beans, black, mature seeds, cooked, boiled, without salt

Beans, great northern, mature seeds, cooked, boiled, without salt

Beans, kidney, red, mature seeds, canned

Beans, kidney, red, mature seeds, cooked, boiled, without salt

Beans, navy, mature seeds, cooked, boiled, without salt

Beans, pinto, mature seeds, cooked, boiled, without salt

Beans, snap, green, canned, regular pack, drained solids

Beans, snap, green, cooked, boiled, drained, without salt

Beans, snap, green, frozen, cooked, boiled, drained without salt

Beans, snap, yellow, canned, regular pack, drained solids

Beans, snap, yellow, cooked, boiled, drained, without salt

Beans, snap, yellow, frozen, cooked, boiled, drained, without salt

Beans, white, mature seeds, canned

Beef stew, canned entree

Beef, chuck, blade roast, separable lean and fat, trimmed to 1/4" fat, all grades, cooked, braised

Beef, chuck, blade roast, separable lean only, trimmed to 1/4" fat, all grades, cooked, braised

Beef, cured, corned beef, canned

Beef, cured, dried

Common Measure	Content per Measure
1 cup	52.121
1 cup	39.860
1 cup	53.079
1 cup	49.057
1 cup	40.781
1 cup	37.329
1 cup	39.910
1 cup	40.356
1 cup	47.884
1 cup	42.494
1 cup	6.075
1 cup	9.850
1 cup	8.708
1 cup	6.075
1 cup	9.850
1 cup	8.708
1 cup	57.483
1 cup	15.706
3 oz	0.000
3 oz	0.000
3 oz	0.000
1 oz	0.782

Description

Beef, chuck, blade roast, separable lean and fat, trimmed to 1/4" fat, all grades, cooked, braised

Beef, chuck, blade roast, separable lean only, trimmed to 1/4" fat, all grades, cooked, braised

Beef, cured, corned beef, canned

Beef, cured, dried

Beef, ground, 75% lean meat / 25% fat, patty, cooked, broiled

Beef, ground, 80% lean meat / 20% fat, patty, cooked, broiled

Beef, ground, 85% lean meat / 15% fat, patty, cooked, broiled

Beef, rib, whole (ribs 6-12), separable lean and fat, trimmed to 1/4" fat, all grades, cooked, roasted

Beef, rib, whole (ribs 6-12), separable lean only, trimmed to 1/4" fat, all grades, cooked, roasted

Beef, round, bottom round, separable lean and fat, trimmed to 1/4" fat, all grades, cooked, braised

Beef, round, bottom round, separable lean only, trimmed to 1/4" fat, all grades, cooked, braised

Beef, round, eye of round, separable lean and fat, trimmed to 1/4" fat, all grades, cooked, roasted

Beef, round, eye of round, separable lean only, trimmed to 1/4" fat, all grades, cooked, roasted

Beef, top sirloin, separable lean and fat, trimmed to 1/4" fat, all grades, cooked, broiled

Beef, top sirloin, separable lean only, trimmed to 1/4" fat, all grades, cooked, broiled

Beef, variety meats and by-products, liver, cooked, pan-fried

Beet greens, cooked, boiled, drained, without salt

Common Measure	Content per Measure
3 oz	0.000
3 oz	0.000
3 oz	0.000
1 oz	0.782
3 oz	0.000
3 oz	0.000
3 oz	0.000
3 oz	0.000
3 oz	0.000
3 oz	0.000
3 oz	0.000
3 oz	0.000
3 oz	0.000
3 oz	0.000
3 oz	0.000
3 oz	4.386
1 cup	7.862

Description

Beets, canned, drained solids

Beets, canned, drained solids

Beets, cooked, boiled, drained

Beets, cooked, boiled, drained

Biscuits, plain or buttermilk, prepared from recipe

Biscuits, plain or buttermilk, prepared from recipe

Biscuits, plain or buttermilk, refrigerated dough, higher fat, baked

Biscuits, plain or buttermilk, refrigerated dough, lower fat, baked

Blackberries, raw

Blueberries, frozen, sweetened

Blueberries, raw

Bologna, beef and pork

Braunschweiger (a liver sausage), pork

Bread crumbs, dry, grated, plain

Bread crumbs, dry, grated, seasoned

Bread stuffing, bread, dry mix, prepared

Bread, banana, prepared from recipe, made with margarine

Bread, cornbread, dry mix, prepared

Bread, cornbread, prepared from recipe, made with low fat (2%) milk

Bread, cracked-wheat

Bread, egg

Bread, french or vienna (includes sourdough)

Bread, indian (navajo) fry

Common Measure	Content per Measure
1 cup	52.121
1 cup	39.860
1 cup	53.079
1 cup	49.057
1 cup	40.781
1 cup	37.329
1 cup	39.910
1 cup	40.356
1 cup	47.884
1 cup	42.494
1 cup	6.075
1 cup	9.850
1 cup	8.708
1 cup	6.075
1 cup	9.850
1 cup	8.708
1 cup	57.483
1 cup	15.706
3 oz	0.000
3 oz	0.000
3 oz	0.000
1 oz	0.782

Description

Bread, indian (navajo) fry

Bread, italian

Bread, mixed-grain (includes whole-grain, 7-grain)

Bread, mixed-grain, toasted (includes whole-grain, 7-grain)

Bread, oatmeal

Bread, oatmeal, toasted

Bread, pita, white, enriched

Bread, pita, white, enriched

Bread, pumpernickel

Bread, pumpernickel, toasted

Bread, raisin, enriched

Bread, raisin, toasted, enriched

Bread, reduced-calorie, rye

Bread, reduced-calorie, wheat

Bread, reduced-calorie, white

Bread, rye

Bread, rye, toasted

Bread, wheat (includes wheat berry)

Bread, wheat, toasted (includes wheat berry)

Bread, white, commercially prepared (includes soft bread crumbs)

Bread, white, commercially prepared (includes soft bread crumbs)

Bread, white, commercially prepared, toasted

Bread, whole-wheat, commercially prepared

Common Measure	Content per Measure
5" bread	47.970
1 slice	10.000
1 slice	12.064
1 slice	12.096
1 slice	13.095
1 slice	13.175
4" pita	15.596
6-1/2" pita	33.420
1 slice	15.200
1 slice	15.138
1 slice	13.598
1 slice	13.656
1 slice	9.315
1 slice	10.028
1 slice	10.189
1 slice	15.456
1 slice	12.744
1 slice	11.800
1 slice	11.799
1 cup	22.775
1 slice	12.653
1 slice	11.968
1 slice	12.908

Description

Bread, whole-wheat, commercially prepared, toasted

Breakfast items, biscuit with egg and sausage

Breakfast items, french toast with butter

Broccoli, cooked, boiled, drained, without salt

Broccoli, cooked, boiled, drained, without salt

Broccoli, flower clusters, raw

Broccoli, frozen, chopped, cooked, boiled, drained, without salt

Broccoli, raw

Broccoli, raw

Brussels sprouts, cooked, boiled, drained, without salt

Brussels sprouts, frozen, cooked, boiled, drained, without salt

Buckwheat flour, whole-groat

Buckwheat groats, roasted, cooked

Bulgur, cooked

Bulgur, dry

Butter, salted

Butter, without salt

Cabbage, chinese (pak-choi), cooked, boiled, drained, without salt

Cabbage, chinese (pe-tsai), cooked, boiled, drained, without salt

Cabbage, cooked, boiled, drained, without salt

Cabbage, raw

Cabbage, red, raw

Cabbage, savoy, raw

Common Measure	Content per Measure
1 slice	12.925
1 biscuit	41.148
2 slices	36.045
1 cup	11.201
1 spear	2.657
1 floweret	0.576
1 cup	9.844
1 cup	5.843
1 spear	2.058
1 cup	11.076
1 cup	12.896
1 cup	84.708
1 cup	33.499
1 cup	33.816
1 cup	106.218
1 tbsp	0.009
1 tbsp	0.009
1 cup	3.026
1 cup	2.868
1 cup	6.690
1 cup	3.906
1 cup	5.159
1 cup	4.270

Description

Cabbage, raw

Cabbage, red, raw

Cabbage, savoy, raw

Cake, angelfood, commercially prepared

Cake, angelfood, dry mix, prepared

Cake, boston cream pie, commercially prepared

Cake, chocolate, commercially prepared with chocolate frosting

Cake, chocolate, prepared from recipe without frosting

Cake, fruitcake, commercially prepared

Cake, gingerbread, prepared from recipe

Cake, pineapple upside-down, prepared from recipe

Cake, pound, commercially prepared, butter

Cake, pound, commercially prepared, fat-free

Cake, shortcake, biscuit-type, prepared from recipe

Cake, snack cakes, creme-filled, chocolate with frosting

Cake, snack cakes, creme-filled, sponge

Cake, snack cakes, cupcakes, chocolate, with frosting, low-fat

Cake, sponge, commercially prepared

Cake, sponge, prepared from recipe

Cake, white, prepared from recipe with coconut frosting

Cake, white, prepared from recipe without frosting

Cake, yellow, commercially prepared, with chocolate frosting

Cake, yellow, commercially prepared, with vanilla frosting

Common Measure	Content per Measure
1 cup	3.906
1 cup	5.159
1 cup	4.270
1 piece	16.184
1 piece	29.350
1 piece	39.468
1 piece	34.944
1 piece	50.730
1 piece	26.488
1 piece	36.408
1 piece	58.075
1 piece	13.664
1 slice	17.080
1 shortcake	31.525
1 cupcake	30.150
1 cake	27.158
1 cupcake	28.896
1 shortcake	18.330
1 piece	36.351
1 piece	70.784
1 piece	42.328
1 piece	35.456
1 piece	37.632

Description

Candies, caramels

Candies, caramels, chocolate-flavor roll

Candies, carob

Candies, confectioner's coating, white

Candies, fudge, chocolate, prepared-from-recipe

Candies, fudge, chocolate, with nuts, prepared-from-recipe

Candies, fudge, vanilla with nuts for 19104

Candies, fudge, vanilla, prepared-from-recipe

Candies, gumdrops, starch jelly pieces

Candies, gumdrops, starch jelly pieces

Candies, gumdrops, starch jelly pieces

Candies, hard

Candies, hard

Candies, jellybeans

Candies, KIT KAT Wafer Bar

Candies, M&M MARS, "M&M's" Milk Chocolate Candies

Candies, M&M MARS, "M&M's" Peanut Chocolate Candies

Candies, M&M MARS, MARS MILKY WAY Bar

Candies, M&M MARS, MARS MILKY WAY Bar

Candies, M&M MARS, SNICKERS Bar

Candies, M&M MARS, STARBURST Fruit Chews

Candies, marshmallows

Candies, milk chocolate

Common Measure	Content per Measure
1 piece	7.777
1 piece	5.762
1 oz	15.958
1 cup	100.725
1 piece	13.002
1 piece	12.912
1 piece	11.211
1 piece	13.165
1 medium	4.154
10 worms	73.186
10 bears	21.758
1 piece	5.880
1 small piece	2.940
10 large	26.521
1 bar (1.5 oz)	26.951
10 pieces	4.985
10 pieces	12.092
1 bar (2.15 oz)	43.737
1 fun size bar	12.906
1 bar (2 oz)	33.750
1 piece	4.225
1 cup	40.650
1 bar (1.55 oz)	26.136

Description

Candies, milk chocolate coated peanuts

Candies, milk chocolate coated raisins

Candies, milk chocolate, with almonds

Candies, MR. GOODBAR Chocolate Bar

Candies, NESTLE, BUTTERFINGER Bar

Candies, NESTLE, CRUNCH Bar and Dessert Topping

Candies, REESE'S Peanut Butter Cups

Candies, semisweet chocolate

Candies, SPECIAL DARK Chocolate Bar

Carambola, (starfruit), raw

Carambola, (starfruit), raw

Carbonated beverage, club soda

Carbonated beverage, cola, contains caffeine

Carbonated beverage, ginger ale

Carbonated beverage, grape soda

Carbonated beverage, lemon-lime soda

Carbonated beverage, low calorie, cola or pepper-type, with aspartame, contains caffeine

Carbonated beverage, low calorie, other than cola or pepper, withou caffeine

Carbonated beverage, orange

Carbonated beverage, pepper-type, contains caffeine

Carbonated beverage, root beer

Carob flour

Common Measure	Content per Measure
10 pieces	19.760
10 pieces	6.830
1 bar (1.45 oz)	21.812
1 bar (1.75 oz)	26.627
1 fun size bar	5.074
1 bar (1.55 oz)	28.692
1 package (contains 2)	24.912
1 cup	106.008
1 miniature	4.990
1 cup	8.456
1 fruit	7.125
12 fl oz	0.000
12 fl oz	39.775
12 fl oz	32.098
12 fl oz	41.664
12 fl oz	38.272
12 fl oz	0.355
12 fl oz	0.000
12 fl oz	45.756
12 fl oz	38.272
12 fl oz	39.220
1 tbsp	7.110

Description

Carrot juice, canned

Carrots, baby, raw

Carrots, canned, regular pack, drained solids

Carrots, cooked, boiled, drained, without salt

Carrots, frozen, cooked, boiled, drained, without salt

Carrots, raw

Carrots, raw

Catsup

Catsup

Cauliflower, cooked, boiled, drained, without salt

Cauliflower, cooked, boiled, drained, without salt

Cauliflower, frozen, cooked, boiled, drained, without salt

Cauliflower, raw

Cauliflower, raw

Celery, cooked, boiled, drained, without salt

Celery, cooked, boiled, drained, without salt

Celery, raw

Celery, raw

Cereals ready-to-eat, GENERAL MILLS, APPLE CINNAMON CHEERIOS

Cereals ready-to-eat, GENERAL MILLS, BASIC 4

Cereals ready-to-eat, GENERAL MILLS, BERRY BERRY KIX

Cereals ready-to-eat, GENERAL MILLS, CHEERIOS

Common Measure	Content per Measure
1 cup	21.924
1 medium	0.824
1 cup	8.088
1 cup	12.823
1 cup	11.286
1 carrot	6.898
1 cup	10.538
1 tbsp	3.582
1 packet	1.433
1 cup	5.096
3 flowerets	2.219
1 cup	6.750
1 cup	5.300
1 floweret	0.689
1 stalk	1.504
1 cup	6.015
1 stalk	1.188
1 cup	3.564
3/4 cup	25.200
1 cup	42.350
3/4 cup	26.100
1 cup	22.200

Description

Cereals ready-to-eat, GENERAL MILLS, CINNAMON TOAST CRUNCH

Cereals ready-to-eat, GENERAL MILLS, COCOA PUFFS

Cereals ready-to-eat, GENERAL MILLS, Corn CHEX

Cereals ready-to-eat, GENERAL MILLS, FROSTED WHEATIES

Cereals ready-to-eat, GENERAL MILLS, GOLDEN GRAHAMS

Cereals ready-to-eat, GENERAL MILLS, HONEY NUT CHEERIOS

Cereals ready-to-eat, GENERAL MILLS, Honey Nut CHEX

Cereals ready-to-eat, GENERAL MILLS, HONEY NUT CLUSTERS

Cereals ready-to-eat, GENERAL MILLS, KIX

Cereals ready-to-eat, GENERAL MILLS, LUCKY CHARMS

Cereals ready-to-eat, GENERAL MILLS, RAISIN NUT BRAN

Cereals ready-to-eat, GENERAL MILLS, REESE'S PUFFS

Cereals ready-to-eat, GENERAL MILLS, Rice CHEX

Cereals ready-to-eat, GENERAL MILLS, TOTAL Corn Flakes

Cereals ready-to-eat, GENERAL MILLS, TOTAL Raisin Bran

Cereals ready-to-eat, GENERAL MILLS, TRIX

Cereals ready-to-eat, GENERAL MILLS, Wheat CHEX

Cereals ready-to-eat, GENERAL MILLS, WHEATIES

Cereals ready-to-eat, GENERAL MILLS, Whole Grain TOTAL

Cereals ready-to-eat, KELLOGG, KELLOGG'S ALL-BRAN Original

Cereals ready-to-eat, KELLOGG, KELLOGG'S APPLE JACKS

Cereals ready-to-eat, KELLOGG, KELLOGG'S COCOA KRISPIES

Common Measure	Content per Measure
3/4 cup	23.700
1 cup	26.400
1 cup	25.800
3/4 cup	26.700
3/4 cup	24.900
1 cup	24.000
3/4 cup	26.100
1 cup	45.650
1-1/3 cup	25.800
1 cup	24.900
1 cup	41.454
3/4 cup	23.400
1-1/4 cup	26.660
1-1/3 cup	25.665
1 cup	41.250
1 cup	26.700
1 cup	24.300
1 cup	24.300
3/4 cup	22.500
1/2 cup	22.200
1 cup	27.300
3/4 cup	27.001

Description

Cereals ready-to-eat, KELLOGG, KELLOGG'S Complete Wheat Bran Flakes

Cereals ready-to-eat, KELLOGG, KELLOGG'S Corn Flakes

Cereals ready-to-eat, KELLOGG, KELLOGG'S CORN POPS

Cereals ready-to-eat, KELLOGG, KELLOGG'S CRISPIX

Cereals ready-to-eat, KELLOGG, KELLOGG'S FROOT LOOPS

Cereals ready-to-eat, KELLOGG, KELLOGG'S FROSTED FLAKES

Cereals ready-to-eat, KELLOGG, KELLOGG'S FROSTED MINI-WHEATS, bite size

Cereals ready-to-eat, KELLOGG, KELLOGG'S PRODUCT 19

Cereals ready-to-eat, KELLOGG, KELLOGG'S RAISIN BRAN

Cereals ready-to-eat, KELLOGG, KELLOGG'S RICE KRISPIES

Cereals ready-to-eat, KELLOGG, KELLOGG'S RICE KRISPIES TREATS Cereal

Cereals ready-to-eat, KELLOGG, KELLOGG'S SMACKS

Cereals ready-to-eat, KELLOGG, KELLOGG'S SPECIAL K

Cereals ready-to-eat, KELLOGG'S FROSTED MINI-WHEATS, original

Cereals ready-to-eat, KRAFT, POST THE ORIGINAL SHREDDED WHEAT Cereal

Cereals ready-to-eat, QUAKER, CAP'N CRUNCH

Cereals ready-to-eat, QUAKER, CAP'N CRUNCH with CRUNCHBERRIES

Cereals ready-to-eat, QUAKER, CAP'N CRUNCH'S PEANUT BUTTER CRUNCH

Cereals ready-to-eat, QUAKER, Honey Nut Heaven

Common Measure	Content per Measure
3/4 cup	22.910
1 cup	24.080
1 cup	27.900
1 cup	24.940
1 cup	26.250
3/4 cup	27.993
1 cup	44.550
1 cup	24.900
1 cup	46.543
1-1/4 cup	29.040
3/4 cup	26.100
3/4 cup	24.030
1 cup	22.010
1 cup	41.004
2 biscuits	38.134
3/4 cup	22.901
3/4 cup	22.118
3/4 cup	21.257
1 cup	37.926

Description

Cereals ready-to-eat, QUAKER, Low Fat 100% Natural Granola with Raisins

Cereals ready-to-eat, QUAKER, QUAKER 100% Natural Cereal with oats, honey, and raisins

Cereals ready-to-eat, QUAKER, QUAKER OAT CINNAMON LIFE

Cereals ready-to-eat, QUAKER, QUAKER OAT LIFE, plain

Cereals ready-to-eat, rice, puffed, fortified

Cereals ready-to-eat, wheat germ, toasted, plain

Cereals ready-to-eat, wheat, puffed, fortified

Cereals, corn grits, white, regular and quick, enriched, cooked with water, without salt

Cereals, corn grits, yellow, regular and quick, enriched, cooked with water, without salt

Cereals, CREAM OF WHEAT, mix'n eat, plain, prepared with water

Cereals, CREAM OF WHEAT, quick, cooked with water, without salt

Cereals, CREAM OF WHEAT, regular, cooked with water, without salt

Cereals, MALT-O-MEAL, plain and chocolate, cooked with water, without salt

Cereals, oats, instant, fortified, plain, prepared with water

Cereals, oats, regular and quick and instant, unenriched, cooked with water, without salt

Cereals, QUAKER, corn grits, instant, plain, prepared with water

Cereals, QUAKER, Instant Oatmeal, maple and brown sugar, prepared with boiling water

Cereals, QUAKER,Instant Oatmeal, apples and cinnamon, prepared with boiling water

Common Measure	Content per Measure
1/2 cup	40.590
1/2 cup	33.527
3/4 cup	25.485
3/4 cup	24.992
1 cup	12.572
1 tbsp	3.531
1 cup	9.552
1 cup	31.145
1 cup	31.145
1 packet	21.442
1 cup	26.768
1 cup	26.932
1 cup	25.680
1 packet	16.974
1 cup	25.272
1 packet	20.632
1 packet	31.062
1 packet	26.477

Description

Cereals, WHEATENA, cooked with water

Cheese food, pasteurized process, american, without di sodium phosphate

Cheese sauce, prepared from recipe

Cheese spread, pasteurized process, american, without di sodium phosphate

Cheese, blue

Cheese, camembert

Cheese, cheddar

Cheese, cottage, creamed, large or small curd

Cheese, cottage, creamed, with fruit

Cheese, cottage, lowfat, 1% milkfat

Cheese, cottage, lowfat, 2% milkfat

Cheese, cottage, nonfat, uncreamed, dry, large or small curd

Cheese, cream

Cheese, cream, fat free

Cheese, feta

Cheese, low fat, cheddar or colby

Cheese, mozzarella, part skim milk, low moisture

Cheese, mozzarella, whole milk

Cheese, muenster

Cheese, neufchatel

Cheese, parmesan, grated

Cheese, pasteurized process, american, with di sodium phosphate

Common Measure	Content per Measure
1 cup	28.674
1 oz	2.220
1 cup	13.316
1 oz	2.475
1 oz	0.663
1 wedge	0.175
1 oz	0.363
1 cup	5.628
1 cup	10.419
1 cup	6.147
1 cup	8.204
1 cup	2.683
1 tbsp	0.386
1 tbsp	0.905
1 oz	1.160
1 oz	0.541
1 oz	1.086
1 oz	0.621
1 oz	0.318
1 oz	0.833
1 tbsp	0.203
1 oz	0.454

Description

Cheese, pasteurized process, swiss, with di sodium phosphate

Cheese, provolone

Cheese, ricotta, part skim milk

Cheese, ricotta, whole milk

Cheese, swiss

Cheesecake commercially prepared

Cherries, sour, red, canned, water pack, solids and liquids (includes USDA commodity red tart cherries, canned)

Cherries, sweet, raw

Chicken pot pie, frozen entree

Chicken roll, light meat

Chicken, broilers or fryers, breast, meat and skin, cooked, fried, batter

Chicken, broilers or fryers, breast, meat and skin, cooked, fried, flour

Chicken, broilers or fryers, breast, meat only, cooked, roasted

Chicken, broilers or fryers, dark meat, meat only, cooked, fried

Chicken, broilers or fryers, drumstick, meat and skin, cooked, fried, batter

Chicken, broilers or fryers, drumstick, meat and skin, cooked, fried, flour

Chicken, broilers or fryers, drumstick, meat only, cooked, roasted

Chicken, broilers or fryers, giblets, cooked, simmered

Chicken, broilers or fryers, light meat, meat only, cooked, fried

Chicken, broilers or fryers, neck, meat only, cooked, simmered

Chicken, broilers or fryers, thigh, meat and skin, cooked, fried, batter

Common Measure	Content per Measure
1 oz	0.595
1 oz	0.607
1 cup	12.644
1 cup	7.478
1 oz	1.525
1 piece	20.400
1 cup	21.814
10 cherries	10.887
1 small pie	42.706
2 slices	1.383
1/2 breast	12.586
1/2 breast	1.607
1/2 breast	0.000
3 oz	2.176
1 drumstick	5.962
1 drumstick	0.799
1 drumstick	0.000
1 cup	0.624
3 oz	0.353
1 neck	0.000
1 thigh	7.809

Description

Chicken, broilers or fryers, thigh, meat only, cooked, roasted

Chicken, broilers or fryers, wing, meat and skin, cooked, fried, batter

Chicken, canned, meat only, with broth

Chicken, liver, all classes, cooked, simmered

Chicken, stewing, meat only, cooked, stewed

Chickpeas (garbanzo beans, bengal gram), mature seeds, canned

Chickpeas (garbanzo beans, bengal gram), mature seeds, cooked, boiled, without salt

Chili con carne with beans, canned entree

Chives, raw

Chocolate syrup

Chocolate-flavor beverage mix for milk, powder, without added nutrients

Chocolate-flavor beverage mix, powder, prepared with whole milk

Cocoa mix, no sugar added, powder

Cocoa mix, powder

Cocoa mix, powder, prepared with water

Cocoa mix, with aspartame, powder, prepared from item 14196

Cocoa, dry powder, unsweetened

Coffee, brewed from grounds, prepared with tap water

Coffee, brewed, espresso, restaurant-prepared

Coffee, instant, regular, prepared with water

Coffeecake, cinnamon with crumb topping, commercially prepared, enriched

Common Measure	Content per Measure
1 thigh	0.000
1 wing	5.361
5 oz	0.000
1 liver	0.171
1 cup	0.000
1 cup	54.288
1 cup	44.969
1 cup	24.487
1 tbsp	0.131
1 tbsp	12.206
2-3 heaping tsp	19.505
1 cup	31.681
1/2 oz envelope	10.460
3 heaping tsp	23.961
1 serving	23.978
1 serving	10.445
1 tbsp	2.932
6 fl oz	0.000
2 fl oz	0.918
6 fl oz	0.609
1 piece	29.421

Description

Coleslaw, home-prepared

Collards, cooked, boiled, drained, without salt

Collards, frozen, chopped, cooked, boiled, drained, without salt

Cookies, brownies, commercially prepared

Cookies, brownies, dry mix, special dietary, prepared

Cookies, butter, commercially prepared, enriched

Cookies, chocolate chip, commercially prepared, reg, higher fat, enriched

Cookies, chocolate chip, commercially prepared, regular, lower fat

Cookies, chocolate chip, prepared from recipe, made with margarine

Cookies, chocolate chip, refrigerated dough, baked

Cookies, chocolate sandwich, with creme filling, regular

Cookies, fig bars

Cookies, graham crackers, plain or honey (includes cinnamon)

Cookies, graham crackers, plain or honey (includes cinnamon)

Cookies, molasses

Cookies, molasses

Cookies, oatmeal, commercially prepared, fat-free

Cookies, oatmeal, commercially prepared, regular

Cookies, oatmeal, commercially prepared, soft-type

Cookies, oatmeal, prepared from recipe, with raisins

Cookies, peanut butter, commercially prepared, regular

Cookies, peanut butter, prepared from recipe

Common Measure	Content per Measure
1 cup	14.892
1 cup	9.329
1 cup	12.087
1 brownie	35.784
1 brownie	15.686
1 cookie	3.445
1 cookie	6.680
1 cookie	7.330
1 cookie	9.344
1 cookie	17.732
1 cookie	7.030
1 cookie	11.344
1 cup	64.512
2 squares	10.752
1 cookie, medium	11.070
1 cookie, large (3-1/2" to 4"	23.616
1 cookie	8.646
1 cookie	17.175
1 cookie	9.855
1 cookie	10.260
1 cookie	8.835
1 cookie	11.780

Description

Cookies, shortbread, commercially prepared, pecan

Cookies, shortbread, commercially prepared, plain

Cookies, sugar, commercially prepared, regular (includes vanilla)

Cookies, sugar, prepared from recipe, made with margarine

Cookies, sugar, refrigerated dough, baked

Cookies, vanilla sandwich with creme filling

Cookies, vanilla sandwich with creme filling

Cookies, vanilla wafers, lower fat

Corn, sweet, white, cooked, boiled, drained, without salt

Corn, sweet, yellow, canned, cream style, regular pack

Corn, sweet, yellow, canned, vacuum pack, regular pack

Corn, sweet, yellow, cooked, boiled, drained, without salt

Corn, sweet, yellow, frozen, kernels cut off cob, boiled, drained, without salt

Corn, sweet, yellow, frozen, kernels on cob, cooked, boiled, drained, without salt

Cornmeal, degermed, enriched, yellow

Cornmeal, self-rising, degermed, enriched, yellow

Cornmeal, whole-grain, yellow

Cornstarch

Couscous, cooked

Couscous, dry

Cowpeas (Blackeyes), immature seeds, cooked, boiled, drained, without salt

Common Measure	Content per Measure
1 cookie	8.162
1 cookie	5.160
1 cookie	10.185
1 cookie	8.400
1 cookie	9.840
1 cookie	7.210
1 cookie	10.815
1 cookie	2.944
1 ear	19.335
1 cup	46.413
1 cup	40.824
1 ear	19.335
1 cup	31.652
1 ear	14.068
1 cup	107.198
1 cup	103.210
1 cup	93.806
1 tbsp	7.360
1 cup	36.455
1 cup	133.954
1 cup	33.528

Description

Cowpeas (blackeyes), immature seeds, frozen, cooked, boiled, drained, without salt

Cowpeas, common (blackeyes, crowder, southern), mature seeds, canned, plain

Cowpeas, common (blackeyes, crowder, southern), mature seeds, cooked, boiled, without salt

Crackers, cheese, regular

Crackers, cheese, sandwich-type with peanut butter filling

Crackers, matzo, plain

Crackers, melba toast, plain

Crackers, rye, wafers, plain

Crackers, saltines (includes oyster, soda, soup)

Crackers, standard snack-type, regular

Crackers, standard snack-type, sandwich, with cheese filling

Crackers, wheat, regular

Crackers, whole-wheat

Cranberry juice cocktail, bottled

Cranberry sauce, canned, sweetened

Cream substitute, liquid, with hydrogenated vegetable oil and soy protein

Cream substitute, powdered

Cream, fluid, half and half

Cream, fluid, heavy whipping

Cream, fluid, light (coffee cream or table cream)

Cream, fluid, light whipping

Common Measure	Content per Measure
1 cup	40.392
1 cup	32.712
1 cup	35.707
10 crackers	5.820
1 sandwich	3.972
1 matzo	23.729
4 pieces	15.320
1 wafer	8.844
4 crackers	8.580
4 crackers	7.320
1 sandwich	4.319
4 crackers	5.192
4 crackers	10.976
8 fl oz	36.432
1 slice	22.173
1 tbsp	1.707
1 tsp	1.098
1 tbsp	0.645
1 tbsp	0.419
1 tbsp	0.549
1 tbsp	0.444

Description

Cream, sour, cultured

Cream, sour, reduced fat, cultured

Cream, whipped, cream topping, pressurized

Croissants, butter

Croutons, seasoned

Crustaceans, crab, alaska king, cooked, moist heat

Crustaceans, crab, alaska king, imitation, made from surimi

Crustaceans, crab, blue, canned

Crustaceans, crab, blue, cooked, moist heat

Crustaceans, crab, blue, crab cakes

Crustaceans, lobster, northern, cooked, moist heat

Crustaceans, shrimp, mixed species, canned

Crustaceans, shrimp, mixed species, cooked, breaded and fried

Crustaceans, shrimp, mixed species, cooked, breaded and fried

Cucumber, peeled, raw

Cucumber, peeled, raw

Cucumber, with peel, raw

Cucumber, with peel, raw

Dandelion greens, cooked, boiled, drained, without salt

Danish pastry, cheese

Danish pastry, fruit, enriched (includes apple, cinnamon, raisin, lemon, raspberry, strawberry)

Dates, deglet noor

Common Measure	Content per Measure
1 tbsp	0.512
1 tbsp	0.639
1 tbsp	0.375
1 croissant	26.106
1 cup	25.400
3 oz	0.000
3 oz	8.687
1 cup	0.000
3 oz	0.000
1 cake	0.288
3 oz	1.088
3 oz	0.876
3 oz	9.750
6 large	5.162
1 large	6.048
1 cup	2.570
1 large	10.926
1 cup	3.775
1 cup	6.720
1 danish	26.412
1 danish	33.938
5 dates	31.137

Description

Dates, deglet noor

Dessert topping, powdered, 1.5 ounce prepared with 1/2 cup milk

Dessert topping, pressurized

Dessert topping, semi solid, frozen

Dill weed, fresh

Doughnuts, cake-type, plain (includes unsugared, old-fashioned)

Doughnuts, cake-type, plain (includes unsugared, old-fashioned)

Doughnuts, yeast-leavened, glazed, enriched (includes honey buns)

Doughnuts, yeast-leavened, glazed, enriched (includes honey buns)

Duck, domesticated, meat only, cooked, roasted

Eclairs, custard-filled with chocolate glaze, prepared from recipe

Egg substitute, liquid

Egg, white, raw, fresh

Egg, whole, cooked, fried

Egg, whole, cooked, hard-boiled

Egg, whole, cooked, poached

Egg, whole, cooked, scrambled

Egg, whole, raw, fresh

Egg, whole, raw, fresh

Egg, whole, raw, fresh

Egg, yolk, raw, fresh

Eggnog

Eggplant, cooked, boiled, drained, without salt

Common Measure	Content per Measure
1 cup	133.553
1 tbsp	0.661
1 tbsp	0.643
1 tbsp	0.922
5 sprigs	0.070
1 medium	23.359
1 hole	6.958
1 hole	5.759
1 medium	26.580
1/2 duck	0.000
1 eclair	24.200
1/4 cup	0.402
1 large	0.244
1 large	0.405
1 large	0.560
1 large	0.380
1 large	1.342
1 large	0.385
1 extra large	0.447
1 medium	0.339
1 large	0.596
1 cup	34.392
1 cup	8.643

Description

Endive, raw

English muffins, plain, enriched, with ca prop (includes sourdough)

English muffins, plain, toasted, enriched, with calcium propionate (includes sourdough)

Entrees, fish fillet, battered or breaded, and fried

Entrees, pizza with cheese

Entrees, pizza with cheese, meat, and vegetables

Entrees, pizza with pepperoni

Fast foods, burrito, with beans and cheese

Fast foods, burrito, with beans and meat

Fast foods, cheeseburger, large, single patty, with condiments and vegetables

Fast foods, cheeseburger, regular, double patty and bun, plain

Fast foods, cheeseburger, regular, double patty, plain

Fast foods, cheeseburger, regular, double patty, with condiments and vegetables

Fast foods, cheeseburger, regular, single patty, with condiments

Fast foods, chicken fillet sandwich, plain

Fast foods, chicken, breaded and fried, boneless pieces, plain

Fast foods, chili con carne

Fast foods, chimichanga, with beef

Fast foods, clams, breaded and fried

Fast foods, coleslaw

Fast foods, croissant, with egg, cheese, and bacon

Common Measure	Content per Measure
1 cup	1.675
1 muffin	26.220
1 muffin	26.000
1 fillet	15.443
1 slice	20.500
1 slice	21.291
1 slice	19.866
1 burrito	27.482
1 burrito	33.010
1 sandwich	38.391
1 sandwich	44.256
1 sandwich	22.057
1 sandwich	35.192
1 sandwich	26.532
1 sandwich	38.693
6 pieces	15.275
1 cup	21.935
1 chimichanga	42.804
3/4 cup	38.813
3/4 cup	12.751
1 croissant	23.646

Description

Fast foods, danish pastry, cheese

Fast foods, danish pastry, fruit

Fast foods, enchilada, with cheese

Fast foods, english muffin, with egg, cheese, and canadian bacon

Fast foods, fish sandwich, with tartar sauce and cheese

Fast foods, french toast sticks

Fast foods, frijoles with cheese

Fast foods, hamburger, large, double patty, with condiments and vegetables

Fast foods, hamburger, regular, double patty, with condiments

Fast foods, hamburger, regular, single patty, with condiments

Fast foods, hotdog, plain

Fast foods, hotdog, with chili

Fast foods, hotdog, with corn flour coating (corndog)

Fast foods, hush puppies

Fast foods, ice milk, vanilla, soft-serve, with cone

Fast foods, nachos, with cheese

Fast foods, onion rings, breaded and fried

Fast foods, pancakes with butter and syrup

Fast foods, potato, french fried in vegetable oil

Fast foods, potato, french fried in vegetable oil

Fast foods, potato, french fried in vegetable oil

Fast foods, potato, mashed

Common Measure	Content per Measure
1 pastry	28.692
1 pastry	45.064
1 enchilada	28.541
1 muffin	26.742
1 sandwich	47.635
5 sticks	57.852
1 cup	28.707
1 sandwich	40.273
1 sandwich	38.743
1 sandwich	34.249
1 sandwich	18.032
1 sandwich	31.293
1 corn dog	55.790
5 pieces	34.897
1 cone	24.112
6-8 nachos	36.330
8-9 rings	31.324
2 pancakes	90.898
1 medium	53.345
1 small	33.839
1 large	67.279
1/3 cup	12.896

Description

Fast foods, potatoes, hashed brown

Fast foods, roast beef sandwich, plain

Fast foods, salad, vegetable, tossed, without dressing, with cheese and egg

Fast foods, salad, vegetable, tossed, without dressing, with chicken

Fast foods, shrimp, breaded and fried

Fast foods, submarine sandwich, with cold cuts

Fast foods, submarine sandwich, with roast beef

Fast foods, submarine sandwich, with tuna salad

Fast foods, sundae, hot fudge

Fast foods, taco

Fast foods, taco

Fast foods, taco salad

Fast foods, tostada, with beans, beef, and cheese

Figs, dried, uncooked

Fish, catfish, channel, cooked, breaded and fried

Fish, cod, Atlantic, canned, solids and liquid

Fish, cod, Pacific, cooked, dry heat

Fish, fish portions and sticks, frozen, preheated

Fish, fish portions and sticks, frozen, preheated

Fish, flatfish (flounder and sole species), cooked, dry heat

Fish, flatfish (flounder and sole species), cooked, dry heat

Fish, haddock, cooked, dry heat

Common Measure	Content per Measure
1/2 cup	16.150
1 sandwich	33.443
1-1/2 cups	4.752
1-1/2 cups	3.728
6-8 shrimp	40.000
1 sandwich, 6" roll	51.049
1 sandwich, 6" roll	44.302
1 sandwich, 6" roll	55.373
1 sundae	47.669
1 small	26.727
1 large	41.107
1-1/2 cups	23.582
1 tostada	29.655
2 figs	24.271
3 oz	6.834
3 oz	0.000
3 oz	0.000
1 portion (4" x 2" x 1/2")	13.538
1 stick (4" x 1" x 1/2")	6.650
1 fillet	0.000
3 oz	0.000
3 oz	0.000

Description

Fish, halibut, Atlantic and Pacific, cooked, dry heat

Fish, herring, Atlantic, pickled

Fish, ocean perch, Atlantic, cooked, dry heat

Fish, ocean perch, Atlantic, cooked, dry heat

Fish, pollock, walleye, cooked, dry heat

Fish, pollock, walleye, cooked, dry heat

Fish, rockfish, Pacific, mixed species, cooked, dry heat

Fish, rockfish, Pacific, mixed species, cooked, dry heat

Fish, roughy, orange, cooked, dry heat

Fish, salmon, chinook, smoked

Fish, salmon, pink, canned, solids with bone and liquid

Fish, salmon, sockeye, cooked, dry heat

Fish, salmon, sockeye, cooked, dry heat

Fish, sardine, Atlantic, canned in oil, drained solids with bone

Fish, swordfish, cooked, dry heat

Fish, swordfish, cooked, dry heat

Fish, trout, rainbow, farmed, cooked, dry heat

Fish, tuna salad

Fish, tuna, light, canned in oil, drained solids

Fish, tuna, light, canned in water, drained solids

Fish, tuna, white, canned in water, drained solids

Fish, tuna, yellowfin, fresh, cooked, dry heat

Frankfurter, beef

Common Measure	Content per Measure
3 oz	0.000
3 oz	8.199
3 oz	0.000
1 fillet	0.000
3 oz	0.000
1 fillet	0.000
1 fillet	0.000
3 oz	0.000
3 oz	0.000
3 oz	0.000
3 oz	0.000
1/2 fillet	0.000
3 oz	0.000
3 oz	0.000
3 oz	0.000
1 piece	0.000
3 oz	0.000
1 cup	19.291
3 oz	0.000
3 oz	0.000
3 oz	0.000
3 oz	0.000
1 frank	1.827

Description

Frankfurter, beef and pork

Frankfurter, chicken

French toast, frozen, ready-to-heat

French toast, prepared from recipe, made with low fat (2%) milk

Frostings, chocolate, creamy, ready-to-eat

Frostings, vanilla, creamy, ready-to-eat

Frozen juice novelties, fruit and juice bars

Frozen yogurts, chocolate, soft-serve

Frozen yogurts, vanilla, soft-serve

Fruit butters, apple

Fruit cocktail, (peach and pineapple and pear and grape and cherry), canned, heavy syrup, solids and liquids

Fruit cocktail, (peach and pineapple and pear and grape and cherry), canned, juice pack, solids and liquids

Fruit punch drink, with added nutrients, canned

Fruit, mixed, (peach and cherry-sweet and -sour and raspberry and grape and boysenberry), frozen, sweetened

Garlic, raw

Gelatin desserts, dry mix, prepared with water

Gelatin desserts, dry mix, reduced calorie, with aspartame, prepared with water

Grape drink, canned

Grape juice, canned or bottled, unsweetened, without added vitamin C

Grape juice, frozen concentrate, sweetened, diluted with 3 volume water, with added vitamin C

Common Measure	Content per Measure
1 frank	0.774
1 frank	3.056
1 slice	18.939
1 slice	16.250
1/12 package	24.016
1/12 package	25.654
1 bar (2.5 fl oz)	15.554
1/2 cup	17.928
1/2 cup	17.424
1 tbsp	7.271
1 cup	46.897
1 cup	28.108
8 fl oz	29.686
1 cup	60.575
1 clove	0.992
1/2 cup	19.157
1/2 cup	4.937
8 fl oz	28.875
1 cup	37.849
1 cup	31.875

Description

Grape juice, frozen concentrate, sweetened, undiluted, with added vitamin C

Grapefruit juice, pink, raw

Grapefruit juice, white, canned, sweetened

Grapefruit juice, white, canned, unsweetened

Grapefruit juice, white, frozen concentrate, unsweetened, diluted with 3 volume water

Grapefruit juice, white, frozen concentrate, unsweetened, undiluted

Grapefruit juice, white, raw

Grapefruit, raw, pink and red, all areas

Grapefruit, raw, white, all areas

Grapefruit, sections, canned, light syrup pack, solids and liquids

Grapes, red or green (european type varieties, such as, Thompson seedless), raw

Grapes, red or green (european type varieties, such as, Thompson seedless), raw

Gravy, beef, canned

Gravy, chicken, canned

Gravy, mushroom, canned

Gravy, NESTLE, CHEF-MATE Country Sausage Gravy, ready-to-serve

Gravy, turkey, canned

Ham, chopped, not canned

Ham, sliced, extra lean, (approximately 5% fat)

Ham, sliced, regular (approximately 11% fat)

Common Measure	Content per Measure
6-fl-oz can	95.839
1 cup	22.724
1 cup	27.825
1 cup	22.131
1 cup	24.033
6-fl-oz can	71.539
1 cup	22.724
1/2 grapefruit	13.112
1/2 grapefruit	9.924
1 cup	39.218
10 grapes	9.050
1 cup	28.960
1/4 cup	2.802
1/4 cup	3.225
1/4 cup	3.260
1/4 cup	3.894
1/4 cup	3.040
2 slices	0.000
2 slices	0.550
2 slices	2.172

Description

HEALTHY CHOICE Beef Macaroni, frozen entree

Hearts of palm, canned

Honey

Horseradish, prepared

Hummus, commercial

Ice creams, chocolate

Ice creams, french vanilla, soft-serve

Ice creams, vanilla

Ice creams, vanilla, light

Ice creams, vanilla, rich

Ice novelties, italian, restaurant-prepared

Ice novelties, pop

Jams and preserves

Jellies

Jerusalem-artichokes, raw

Kale, cooked, boiled, drained, without salt

Kale, frozen, cooked, boiled, drained, without salt

KELLOGG'S Eggo Lowfat Homestyle Waffles

Kiwi fruit, (chinese gooseberries), fresh, raw

Kohlrabi, cooked, boiled, drained, without salt

Lamb, domestic, leg, whole (shank and sirloin), separable lean and fat, trimmed to 1/4" fat, choice, cooked, roasted

Lamb, domestic, leg, whole (shank and sirloin), separable lean only, trimmed to 1/4" fat, choice, cooked, roasted

Common Measure	Content per Measure
1 package	33.456
1 piece	1.525
1 tbsp	17.304
1 tsp	0.565
1 tbsp	2.001
1/2 cup	18.612
1/2 cup	19.092
1/2 cup	15.576
1/2 cup	17.642
1/2 cup	16.495
1/2 cup	15.660
1 bar (2 fl oz)	11.151
1 tbsp	13.772
1 tbsp	13.291
1 cup	26.160
1 cup	7.319
1 cup	6.799
1 waffle	15.453
1 medium	11.142
1 cup	11.039
3 oz	0.000
3 oz	0.000

Description

Lamb, domestic, loin, separable lean and fat, trimmed to 1/4" fat, choice, cooked, broiled

Lamb, domestic, loin, separable lean only, trimmed to 1/4" fat, choice, cooked, broiled

Lamb, domestic, rib, separable lean and fat, trimmed to 1/4" fat, choice, cooked, roasted

Lamb, domestic, rib, separable lean only, trimmed to 1/4" fat, choice, cooked, roasted

Lamb, domestic, shoulder, arm, separable lean and fat, trimmed to 1/4" fat, choice, cooked, braised

Lamb, domestic, shoulder, arm, separable lean only, trimmed to 1/4" fat, choice, cooked, braised

Lard

Leavening agents, baking powder, double-acting, sodium aluminum sulfate

Leavening agents, baking powder, double-acting, straight phosphate

Leavening agents, baking powder, low-sodium

Leavening agents, baking soda

Leavening agents, cream of tartar

Leavening agents, yeast, baker's, active dry

Leavening agents, yeast, baker's, active dry

Leavening agents, yeast, baker's, compressed

Leeks, (bulb and lower leaf-portion), cooked, boiled, drained, withou salt

Lemon juice, canned or bottled

Lemon juice, canned or bottled

Lemon juice, raw

Common Measure	Content per Measure
3 oz	0.000
3 oz	0.000
3 oz	0.000
3 oz	0.000
3 oz	0.000
3 oz	0.000
1 tbsp	0.000
1 tsp	1.274
1 tsp	1.109
1 tsp	2.345
1 tsp	0.000
1 tsp	1.845
1 pkg	2.674
1 tsp	1.528
1 cake	3.077
1 cup	7.925
1 cup	15.811
1 tbsp	0.985
juice of 1 lemon	4.056

Description

Lemonade, frozen concentrate, white, prepared with water

Lemonade, low calorie, with aspartame, powder, prepared with water

Lemonade-flavor drink, powder, prepared with water

Lemons, raw, without peel

Lentils, mature seeds, cooked, boiled, without salt

Lettuce, butterhead (includes boston and bibb types), raw

Lettuce, butterhead (includes boston and bibb types), raw

Lettuce, cos or romaine, raw

Lettuce, cos or romaine, raw

Lettuce, green leaf, raw

Lettuce, green leaf, raw

Lettuce, iceberg (includes crisphead types), raw

Lettuce, iceberg (includes crisphead types), raw

Lettuce, iceberg (includes crisphead types), raw

Lima beans, immature seeds, frozen, baby, cooked, boiled, drained, without salt

Lima beans, immature seeds, frozen, fordhook, cooked, boiled, drained, without salt

Lima beans, large, mature seeds, canned

Lima beans, large, mature seeds, cooked, boiled, without salt

Lime juice, canned or bottled, unsweetened

Lime juice, canned or bottled, unsweetened

Lime juice, raw

Macaroni and Cheese, canned entree

Common Measure	Content per Measure
8 fl oz	34.050
8 fl oz	1.232
8 fl oz	28.728
1 lemon	5.406
1 cup	39.857
1 head	3.635
1 medium leaf	0.167
1 leaf	0.329
1 cup	1.842
1 cup	1.562
1 leaf	0.279
1 head	11.265
1 cup	1.150
1 medium	0.167
1 cup	35.010
1 cup	32.844
1 cup	35.933
1 cup	39.254
1 cup	16.457
1 tbsp	1.030
juice of 1 lime	3.424
1 cup	28.980

Description

Macaroni, cooked, enriched

Malted drink mix, chocolate, with added nutrients, powder

Malted drink mix, chocolate, with added nutrients, powder, prepared with whole milk

Malted drink mix, natural, with added nutrients, powder

Malted drink mix, natural, with added nutrients, powder, prepared with whole milk

Mangos, raw

Mangos, raw

Margarine, regular, tub, composite, 80% fat, with salt

Margarine, regular, unspecified oils, with salt added

Margarine, vegetable oil spread, 60% fat, stick

Margarine, vegetable oil spread, 60% fat, stick

Margarine, vegetable oil spread, 60% fat, tub/bottle

Margarine-butter blend, 60% corn oil margarine and 40% butter

Margarine-like spread, (approximately 40% fat), unspecified oils

Melons, cantaloupe, raw

Melons, cantaloupe, raw

Melons, honeydew, raw

Melons, honeydew, raw

Milk shakes, thick chocolate

Milk shakes, thick vanilla

Milk, buttermilk, dried

Milk, buttermilk, fluid, cultured, lowfat

Common Measure	Content per Measure
1 cup	39.676
3 heaping tsp	17.724
1 cup	28.938
4-5 heaping tsp	17.052
1 cup	28.276
1 cup	28.050
1 mango	35.190
1 tbsp	0.085
1 tbsp	0.127
1 tsp	0.007
1 tbsp	0.020
1 tsp	0.000
1 tbsp	0.092
1 tsp	0.019
1 cup	13.056
1/8 melon	5.630
1/8 melon	14.544
1 cup	15.453
10.6 fl oz	63.450
11 fl oz	55.558
1 tbsp	3.185
1 cup	11.736

Description

Milk, canned, condensed, sweetened

Milk, canned, evaporated, nonfat

Milk, canned, evaporated, without added vitamin A

Milk, chocolate, fluid, commercial,

Milk, chocolate, fluid, commercial, lowfat

Milk, chocolate, fluid, commercial, reduced fat

Milk, dry, nonfat, instant, with added vitamin A

Milk, lowfat, fluid, 1% milkfat, with added vitamin A

Milk, nonfat, fluid, with added vitamin A (fat free or skim)

Milk, reduced fat, fluid, 2% milkfat, with added vitamin A

Milk, whole, 3.25% milkfat

Miso

Molasses, blackstrap

Mollusks, clam, mixed species, canned, drained solids

Mollusks, clam, mixed species, raw

Mollusks, oyster, eastern, cooked, breaded and fried

Mollusks, oyster, eastern, wild, raw

Mollusks, scallop, mixed species, cooked, breaded and fried

Muffins, blueberry, commercially prepared

Muffins, blueberry, prepared from recipe, made with low fat (2%) milk

Muffins, corn, commercially prepared

Muffins, corn, dry mix, prepared

Common Measure	Content per Measure
1 cup	166.464
1 cup	29.056
1 cup	25.301
1 cup	25.850
1 cup	26.100
1 cup	26.000
1/3 cup	12.004
1 cup	12.176
1 cup	12.152
1 cup	11.419
1 cup	11.029
1 cup	19.223
1 tbsp	12.160
3 oz	4.361
3 oz	2.185
3 oz	9.877
6 medium	3.284
6 large	9.421
1 muffin	27.360
1 muffin	23.199
1 muffin	29.013
1 muffin	24.550

Description

Muffins, oat bran

Muffins, wheat bran, toaster-type with raisins, toasted

Mung beans, mature seeds, sprouted, cooked, boiled, drained, withou salt

Mung beans, mature seeds, sprouted, raw

Mushrooms, canned, drained solids

Mushrooms, cooked, boiled, drained, without salt

Mushrooms, raw

Mushrooms, shiitake, cooked, without salt

Mushrooms, shiitake, dried

Mustard greens, cooked, boiled, drained, without salt

Mustard, prepared, yellow

NABISCO, NABISCO SNACKWELL'S Fat Free Devil's Food Cook Cakes

Nectarines, raw

Noodles, chinese, chow mein

Noodles, egg, cooked, enriched

Noodles, egg, spinach, cooked, enriched

Nuts, almonds

Nuts, brazilnuts, dried, unblanched

Nuts, cashew nuts, dry roasted, with salt added

Nuts, cashew nuts, oil roasted, with salt added

Nuts, chestnuts, european, roasted

Nuts, coconut meat, dried (desiccated), sweetened, shredded

Common Measure	Content per Measure
1 muffin	27.531
1 muffin	18.870
1 cup	5.196
1 cup	6.178
1 cup	7.940
1 cup	8.252
1 cup	2.268
1 cup	20.706
1 mushroom	2.713
1 cup	2.940
1 tsp or 1 packet	0.389
1 cookie	11.880
1 nectarine	14.348
1 cup	25.893
1 cup	39.744
1 cup	38.800
1 oz (24 nuts)	5.596
1 oz (6-8 nuts)	3.479
1 oz	9.268
1 oz (18 nuts)	8.550
1 cup	75.733
1 cup	44.333

Description

Nuts, coconut meat, raw

Nuts, hazelnuts or filberts

Nuts, macadamia nuts, dry roasted, with salt added

Nuts, mixed nuts, dry roasted, with peanuts, with salt added

Nuts, mixed nuts, oil roasted, with peanuts, with salt added

Nuts, pecans

Nuts, pine nuts, pignolia, dried

Nuts, pine nuts, pignolia, dried

Nuts, pistachio nuts, dry roasted, with salt added

Nuts, walnuts, english

Oat bran, cooked

Oat bran, raw

Oil, olive, salad or cooking

Oil, peanut, salad or cooking

Oil, sesame, salad or cooking

Oil, soybean, salad or cooking, (hydrogenated)

Oil, soybean, salad or cooking, (hydrogenated) and cottonseed

Oil, vegetable corn, salad or cooking

Oil, vegetable safflower, salad or cooking, oleic, over 70% (primary safflower oil of commerce)

Oil, vegetable, sunflower, linoleic, (60% and over)

Okra, cooked, boiled, drained, without salt

Okra, frozen, cooked, boiled, drained, without salt

Common Measure	Content per Measure
1 piece	6.854
1 oz	4.734
1 oz (10-12 nuts)	3.637
1 oz	7.187
1 oz	6.070
1 oz (20 halves)	3.929
1 oz	3.708
1 tbsp	1.125
1 oz (47 nuts)	7.592
1 oz (14 halves)	3.887
1 cup	25.054
1 cup	62.247
1 tbsp	0.000
1 tbsp	0.000
1 tbsp	0.000
1 tbsp	0.000
1 tbsp	0.000
1 tbsp	0.000
1 tbsp	0.000
1 tbsp	0.000
1 cup	7.280
1 cup	10.580

Description

Olives, ripe, canned (small-extra large)

Onion rings, breaded, par fried, frozen, prepared, heated in oven

Onions, cooked, boiled, drained, without salt

Onions, cooked, boiled, drained, without salt

Onions, dehydrated flakes

Onions, raw

Onions, raw

Onions, raw

Onions, spring or scallions (includes tops and bulb), raw

Onions, spring or scallions (includes tops and bulb), raw

Orange juice, canned, unsweetened

Orange juice, chilled, includes from concentrate

Orange juice, frozen concentrate, unsweetened, diluted with 3 volume water

Orange juice, frozen concentrate, unsweetened, undiluted

Orange juice, raw

Orange juice, raw

Oranges, raw, all commercial varieties

Oranges, raw, all commercial varieties

Pancakes plain, frozen, ready-to-heat (includes buttermilk)

Pancakes, plain, dry mix, complete, prepared

Pancakes, plain, dry mix, incomplete, prepared

Papayas, raw

Common Measure	Content per Measure
5 large	1.377
10 rings	22.896
1 cup	21.315
1 medium	9.541
1 tbsp	4.164
1 whole	11.121
1 slice	1.415
1 cup	16.176
1 cup	7.340
1 whole	1.101
1 cup	24.527
1 cup	25.049
1 cup	26.842
6-fl-oz can	81.302
juice from 1 orange	8.944
1 cup	25.792
1 orange	15.393
1 cup	21.150
1 pancake	15.696
1 pancake	13.946
1 pancake	10.982
1 papaya	29.822

Description

Papayas, raw

Parsley, raw

Parsnips, cooked, boiled, drained, without salt

Pasta with meatballs in tomato sauce, canned entree

Peaches, canned, heavy syrup pack, solids and liquids

Peaches, canned, heavy syrup pack, solids and liquids

Peaches, canned, juice pack, solids and liquids

Peaches, canned, juice pack, solids and liquids

Peaches, dried, sulfured, uncooked

Peaches, frozen, sliced, sweetened

Peaches, raw

Peaches, raw

Peanut butter, chunk style, with salt

Peanut butter, smooth style, with salt

Peanuts, all types, dry-roasted, with salt

Peanuts, all types, dry-roasted, without salt

Peanuts, all types, oil-roasted, with salt

Pears, asian, raw

Pears, asian, raw

Pears, canned, heavy syrup pack, solids and liquids

Pears, canned, heavy syrup pack, solids and liquids

Pears, canned, juice pack, solids and liquids

Pears, canned, juice pack, solids and liquids

Common Measure	Content per Measure
1 cup	13.734
10 sprigs	0.633
1 cup	26.536
1 cup	30.971
1 half	19.541
1 cup	52.243
1 half	11.339
1 cup	28.694
3 halves	23.919
1 cup	59.950
1 peach	9.349
1 cup	16.218
1 tbsp	3.374
1 tbsp	2.947
1 oz (approx 28)	6.098
1 oz (approx 28)	6.098
1 oz	4.326
1 pear	12.993
1 pear	29.288
1 half	14.569
1 cup	50.992
1 cup	32.091
1 half	9.834

Description

Pears, raw

Peas, edible-podded, cooked, boiled, drained, without salt

Peas, edible-podded, frozen, cooked, boiled, drained, without salt

Peas, green, canned, regular pack, drained solids

Peas, green, frozen, cooked, boiled, drained, without salt

Peas, split, mature seeds, cooked, boiled, without salt

Peppers, hot chili, green, raw

Peppers, hot chili, red, raw

Peppers, jalapeno, canned, solids and liquids

Peppers, sweet, green, cooked, boiled, drained, without salt

Peppers, sweet, green, raw

Peppers, sweet, green, raw

Peppers, sweet, green, raw

Peppers, sweet, red, cooked, boiled, drained, without salt

Peppers, sweet, red, raw

Peppers, sweet, red, raw

Pickle relish, sweet

Pickles, cucumber, dill

Pie crust, cookie-type, prepared from recipe, graham cracker, baked

Pie crust, standard-type, frozen, ready-to-bake, baked

Pie crust, standard-type, prepared from recipe, baked

Pie fillings, apple, canned

Pie fillings, canned, cherry

Common Measure	Content per Measure
1 pear	25.664
1 cup	11.280
1 cup	14.432
1 cup	21.386
1 cup	22.816
1 cup	41.356
1 pepper	4.257
1 pepper	3.668
1/4 cup	1.232
1 cup	9.112
1 cup	6.914
1 ring	0.464
1 pepper	5.522
1 cup	9.112
1 pepper	7.176
1 cup	8.985
1 tbsp	5.258
1 pickle	2.678
1 pie shell	155.828
1 pie shell	62.496
1 pie shell	85.500
1/8 of 21-oz can	19.388
1/8 of 21-oz can	20.720

Description

Pie, apple, commercially prepared, enriched flour

Pie, apple, prepared from recipe

Pie, blueberry, commercially prepared

Pie, blueberry, prepared from recipe

Pie, cherry, commercially prepared

Pie, cherry, prepared from recipe

Pie, chocolate creme, commercially prepared

Pie, coconut custard, commercially prepared

Pie, fried pies, cherry

Pie, fried pies, fruit

Pie, lemon meringue, commercially prepared

Pie, lemon meringue, prepared from recipe

Pie, pecan, commercially prepared

Pie, pecan, prepared from recipe

Pie, pumpkin, commercially prepared

Pie, pumpkin, prepared from recipe

Pimento, canned

Pineapple and grapefruit juice drink, canned

Pineapple and orange juice drink, canned

Pineapple juice, canned, unsweetened, without added ascorbic acid

Pineapple, canned, heavy syrup pack, solids and liquids

Pineapple, canned, heavy syrup pack, solids and liquids

Pineapple, canned, juice pack, solids and liquids

Common Measure	Content per Measure
1 piece	39.780
1 piece	57.505
1 piece	40.833
1 piece	49.245
1 piece	46.566
1 piece	69.300
1 piece	37.968
1 piece	31.408
1 pie	54.528
1 pie	54.528
1 piece	53.336
1 piece	49.657
1 piece	64.636
1 piece	63.684
1 piece	29.757
1 piece	40.920
1 tbsp	0.612
8 fl oz	29.000
8 fl oz	29.500
1 cup	34.450
1 slice	9.898
1 cup	51.308
1 slice	7.379

Description

Pineapple, canned, juice pack, solids and liquids

Pineapple, raw, all varieties

Plantains, cooked

Plantains, raw

Plums, canned, purple, heavy syrup pack, solids and liquids

Plums, canned, purple, heavy syrup pack, solids and liquids

Plums, canned, purple, juice pack, solids and liquids

Plums, canned, purple, juice pack, solids and liquids

Plums, dried (prunes), stewed, without added sugar

Plums, dried (prunes), uncooked

Plums, raw

Pork and beef sausage, fresh, cooked

Pork sausage, fresh, cooked

Pork sausage, fresh, cooked

Pork, cured, bacon, cooked, broiled, pan-fried or roasted

Pork, cured, canadian-style bacon, grilled

Pork, cured, ham, extra lean and regular, canned, roasted

Pork, cured, ham, whole, separable lean and fat, roasted

Pork, cured, ham, whole, separable lean only, roasted

Pork, fresh, backribs, separable lean and fat, cooked, roasted

Pork, fresh, leg (ham), whole, separable lean and fat, cooked, roasted

Pork, fresh, leg (ham), whole, separable lean only, cooked, roasted

Pork, fresh, loin, center loin (chops), bone-in, separable lean and fat, cooked, broiled

Common Measure	Content per Measure
1 cup	39.093
1 cup	19.577
1 cup	47.971
1 medium	57.083
1 cup	59.959
1 plum	10.690
1 plum	6.969
1 cup	38.178
1 cup	69.638
5 prunes	26.830
1 plum	7.537
2 links	0.702
2 links	0.000
1 patty	0.000
3 medium slices	0.272
2 slices	0.628
3 oz	0.417
3 oz	0.000
3 oz	0.000
3 oz	0.000
3 oz	0.000
3 oz	0.000
3 oz	0.000

Description

Pork, fresh, loin, center loin (chops), bone-in, separable lean only, cooked, broiled

Pork, fresh, loin, center loin (chops), bone-in, separable lean only, cooked, pan-fried

Pork, fresh, loin, center rib (roasts), bone-in, separable lean and fat, cooked, roasted

Pork, fresh, loin, center rib (roasts), bone-in, separable lean only, cooked, roasted

Pork, fresh, loin, country-style ribs, separable lean and fat, cooked, braised

Pork, fresh, shoulder, arm picnic, separable lean and fat, cooked, braised

Pork, fresh, shoulder, arm picnic, separable lean only, cooked, braised

Pork, fresh, spareribs, separable lean and fat, cooked, braised

Potato pancakes, home-prepared

Potato puffs, frozen, prepared

Potato salad, home-prepared

Potato, baked, flesh and skin, without salt

Potatoes, au gratin, dry mix, prepared with water, whole milk and butter

Potatoes, au gratin, home-prepared from recipe using butter

Potatoes, baked, flesh, without salt

Potatoes, baked, skin, without salt

Potatoes, boiled, cooked in skin, flesh, without salt

Potatoes, boiled, cooked without skin, flesh, without salt

Potatoes, boiled, cooked without skin, flesh, without salt

Common Measure	Content per Measure
3 oz	0.000
3 oz	0.000
3 oz	0.000
3 oz	0.000
3 oz	0.000
3 oz	0.000
3 oz	0.000
3 oz	0.000
1 pancake	21.766
10 puffs	24.071
1 cup	27.925
1 potato	42.723
1 cup	31.458
1 cup	27.612
1 potato	33.618
1 skin	26.715
1 potato	27.377
1 cup	31.216
1 potato	27.014

Description

Potatoes, french fried, frozen, home-prepared, heated in oven, without salt

Potatoes, hashed brown, frozen, plain, prepared

Potatoes, hashed brown, home-prepared

Potatoes, mashed, dehydrated, prepared from flakes without milk, whole milk and butter added

Potatoes, mashed, home-prepared, whole milk added

Potatoes, mashed, home-prepared, whole milk and margarine added

Potatoes, scalloped, dry mix, prepared with water, whole milk and butter

Potatoes, scalloped, home-prepared with butter

Poultry food products, ground turkey, cooked

Prune juice, canned

Puddings, chocolate, dry mix, instant, prepared with 2% milk

Puddings, chocolate, dry mix, regular, prepared with 2% milk

Puddings, chocolate, ready-to-eat

Puddings, rice, ready-to-eat

Puddings, tapioca, ready-to-eat

Puddings, vanilla, dry mix, regular, prepared with 2% milk

Puddings, vanilla, ready-to-eat

Pumpkin, canned, without salt

Pumpkin, cooked, boiled, drained, without salt

Radishes, raw

Raisins, seedless

Common Measure	Content per Measure
10 strips	15.595
1 patty	8.149
1 cup	54.772
1 cup	22.701
1 cup	36.813
1 cup	35.511
1 cup	31.287
1 cup	26.411
1 patty	0.000
1 cup	44.672
1/2 cup	27.768
1/2 cup	27.761
4 oz	25.990
4 oz	24.948
4 oz	21.922
1/2 cup	25.942
4 oz	24.747
1 cup	19.821
1 cup	12.005
1 radish	0.153
1 cup	114.811

Description

Raisins, seedless

Raspberries, frozen, red, sweetened

Raspberries, raw

Refried beans, canned (includes USDA commodity)

Rhubarb, frozen, cooked, with sugar

Rice beverage, RICE DREAM, canned

Rice, brown, long-grain, cooked

Rice, white, long-grain, parboiled, enriched, cooked

Rice, white, long-grain, parboiled, enriched, dry

Rice, white, long-grain, precooked or instant, enriched, prepared

Rice, white, long-grain, regular, cooked

Rice, white, long-grain, regular, raw, enriched

Rolls, dinner, plain, commercially prepared (includes brown-and-serve)

Rolls, hamburger or hotdog, plain

Rolls, hard (includes kaiser)

Rutabagas, cooked, boiled, drained, without salt

Salad dressing, blue or roquefort cheese dressing, commercial, regular

Salad dressing, french dressing, commercial, regular

Salad dressing, french dressing, reduced fat

Salad dressing, french, home recipe

Salad dressing, home recipe, cooked

Salad dressing, home recipe, vinegar and oil

Common Measure	Content per Measure
1 packet	11.085
1 cup	65.400
1 cup	14.686
1 cup	39.136
1 cup	74.880
1 cup	24.843
1 cup	44.772
1 cup	43.278
1 cup	151.182
1 cup	35.096
1 cup	44.509
1 cup	147.908
1 roll	14.112
1 roll	21.264
1 roll	30.039
1 cup	14.858
1 tbsp	1.132
1 tbsp	2.430
1 tbsp	4.773
1 tbsp	0.476
1 tbsp	2.384
1 tbsp	0.390

Description

Salad dressing, italian dressing, commercial, regular

Salad dressing, italian dressing, reduced fat

Salad dressing, mayonnaise, soybean oil, with salt

Salad dressing, russian dressing

Salad dressing, russian dressing, low calorie

Salad dressing, thousand island dressing, reduced fat

Salad dressing, thousand island, commercial, regular

Salami, cooked, beef and pork

Salami, dry or hard, pork, beef

Salt, table

Sandwich spread, pork, beef

Sandwiches and burgers, cheeseburger, large, single meat patty, with bacon and condiments

Sandwiches and burgers, cheeseburger, regular, single meat patty, plain

Sandwiches and burgers, hamburger, large, single meat patty, with condiments and vegetables

Sauce, barbecue sauce

Sauce, cheese, ready-to-serve

Sauce, hoisin, ready-to-serve

Sauce, homemade, white, medium

Sauce, NESTLE, ORTEGA Mild Nacho Cheese Sauce, ready-to-serve

Sauce, pasta, spaghetti/marinara, ready-to-serve

Sauce, ready-to-serve, pepper or hot

Common Measure	Content per Measure
1 tbsp	1.533
1 tbsp	0.686
1 tbsp	0.538
1 tbsp	1.591
1 tbsp	4.499
1 tbsp	3.395
1 tbsp	2.284
2 slices	1.276
2 slices	0.518
1 tsp	0.000
1 tbsp	1.791
1 sandwich	37.128
1 sandwich	31.753
1 sandwich	40.003
1 tbsp	2.016
1/4 cup	4.303
1 tbsp	7.053
1 cup	22.925
1/4 cup	2.520
1 cup	20.550
1 tsp	0.082

Description

Sauce, ready-to-serve, salsa

Sauce, teriyaki, ready-to-serve

Sauerkraut, canned, solids and liquids

Sausage, Vienna, canned, beef and pork

Seaweed, kelp, raw

Seaweed, spirulina, dried

Seeds, pumpkin and squash seed kernels, roasted, with salt added

Seeds, sesame butter, tahini, from roasted and toasted kernels (most common type)

Seeds, sesame seed kernels, dried (decorticated)

Seeds, sunflower seed kernels, dry roasted, with salt added

Seeds, sunflower seed kernels, dry roasted, with salt added

Shake, fast food, chocolate

Shake, fast food, vanilla

Shallots, raw

Sherbet, orange

Shortening, household, soybean (hydrogenated)-cottonseed (hydrogenated)

Snacks, beef jerky, chopped and formed

Snacks, CHEX mix

Snacks, corn-based, extruded, chips, barbecue-flavor

Snacks, corn-based, extruded, chips, plain

Snacks, corn-based, extruded, puffs or twists, cheese-flavor

Snacks, fruit leather, pieces

Common Measure	Content per Measure
1 tbsp	0.998
1 tbsp	2.871
1 cup	10.101
1 sausage	0.326
2 tbsp	0.957
1 tbsp	0.222
1 oz (142 seeds)	3.807
1 tbsp	3.179
1 tbsp	1.235
1/4 cup	7.702
1 oz	6.824
16 fl oz	68.265
16 fl oz	59.607
1 tbsp	1.680
1/2 cup	22.496
1 tbsp	0.000
1 large piece	2.178
1 oz (about 2/3 cup)	18.456
1 oz	15.933
1 oz	16.131
1 oz	15.252
1 oz	23.956

Description

Snacks, fruit leather, rolls

Snacks, granola bars, hard, plain

Snacks, granola bars, soft, coated, milk chocolate coating, peanut butter

Snacks, granola bars, soft, uncoated, chocolate chip

Snacks, granola bars, soft, uncoated, raisin

Snacks, KELLOGG, KELLOGG'S NUTRI-GRAIN Cereal Bars, fruit

Snacks, KELLOGG, KELLOGG'S RICE KRISPIES TREATS Squares

Snacks, oriental mix, rice-based

Snacks, popcorn, air-popped

Snacks, popcorn, cakes

Snacks, popcorn, caramel-coated, with peanuts

Snacks, popcorn, caramel-coated, without peanuts

Snacks, popcorn, cheese-flavor

Snacks, popcorn, oil-popped

Snacks, pork skins, plain

Snacks, potato chips, barbecue-flavor

Snacks, potato chips, made from dried potatoes, light

Snacks, potato chips, made from dried potatoes, plain

Snacks, potato chips, made from dried potatoes, sour-cream and onion-flavor

Snacks, potato chips, plain, salted

Snacks, potato chips, plain, unsalted

Snacks, potato chips, reduced fat

Common Measure	Content per Measure
1 large	17.997
1 bar	18.257
1 bar	15.139
1 bar	19.590
1 bar	18.824
1 bar	26.973
1 bar	17.710
1 oz (about 1/4 cup)	14.634
1 cup	6.232
1 cake	8.010
1 cup	33.894
1 cup	27.843
1 cup	5.676
1 cup	6.292
1 oz	0.000
1 oz	14.969
1 oz	18.399
1 oz	14.459
1 oz	14.544
1 oz	14.997
1 oz	14.997
1 oz	18.966

Description

Snacks, potato chips, sour-cream-and-onion-flavor

Snacks, pretzels, hard, plain, salted

Snacks, rice cakes, brown rice, plain

Snacks, tortilla chips, nacho-flavor

Snacks, tortilla chips, nacho-flavor, reduced fat

Snacks, tortilla chips, plain

Snacks, trail mix, regular, with chocolate chips, salted nuts and seeds

Snacks, trail mix, tropical

Soup, bean with ham, canned, chunky, ready-to-serve, commercial

Soup, bean with pork, canned, prepared with equal volume water, commercial

Soup, beef broth or bouillon, powder, dry

Soup, beef broth, bouillon, consomme, prepared with equal volume water, commercial

Soup, beef noodle, canned, prepared with equal volume water, commercial

Soup, chicken noodle, canned, chunky, ready-to-serve

Soup, chicken noodle, canned, prepared with equal volume water, commercial

Soup, chicken noodle, dehydrated, prepared with water

Soup, chicken vegetable, canned, chunky, ready-to-serve

Soup, chicken with rice, canned, prepared with equal volume water, commercial

Soup, clam chowder, manhattan, canned, prepared with equal volume water

Common Measure	Content per Measure
1 oz	14.600
10 pretzels	47.520
1 cake	7.335
1 oz	17.690
1 oz	20.299
1 oz	17.832
1 cup	65.554
1 cup	91.840
1 cup	27.119
1 cup	22.795
1 packet	1.419
1 cup	1.759
1 cup	8.979
1 cup	17.040
1 cup	9.351
1 cup	9.259
1 cup	18.888
1 cup	7.158
1 cup	12.224

Description

Soup, clam chowder, new england, canned, prepared with equal volume milk, commercial

Soup, cream of chicken, canned, prepared with equal volume water, commercial

Soup, cream of chicken, prepared with equal volume milk, commercial

Soup, cream of mushroom, canned, prepared with equal volume milk, commercial

Soup, cream of mushroom, canned, prepared with equal volume water, commercial

Soup, minestrone, canned, prepared with equal volume water, commercial

Soup, onion mix, dehydrated, dry form

Soup, onion, dehydrated, prepared with water

Soup, pea, green, canned, prepared with equal volume water, commercial

Soup, PROGRESSO HEALTHY CLASSICS CHICKEN NOODLE, canned, ready-to-serve

Soup, PROGRESSO HEALTHY CLASSICS CHICKEN RICE WITH VEGETABLES, canned, ready-to-serve

Soup, PROGRESSO HEALTHY CLASSICS LENTIL, canned, ready-to-serve

Soup, PROGRESSO HEALTHY CLASSICS MINESTRONE, canned, ready-to-serve

Soup, PROGRESSO HEALTHY CLASSICS NEW ENGLAND CLAM CHOWDER, canned, ready-to-serve

Soup, PROGRESSO HEALTHY CLASSICS VEGETABLE, canned, ready-to-serve

Soup, stock, fish, home-prepared

Soup, tomato, canned, prepared with equal volume milk, commercial

Common Measure	Content per Measure
1 cup	16.616
1 cup	9.272
1 cup	14.979
1 cup	15.004
1 cup	9.296
1 cup	11.231
1 packet	20.869
1 cup	5.068
1 cup	26.500
1 cup	9.433
1 cup	12.500
1 cup	20.304
1 cup	20.340
1 cup	19.788
1 cup	13.233
1 cup	0.000
1 cup	22.295

Description

Soup, tomato, canned, prepared with equal volume water, commercial

Soup, vegetable beef, prepared with equal volume water, commercial

Soup, vegetable, canned, chunky, ready-to-serve, commercial

Soup, vegetarian vegetable, canned, prepared with equal volume water, commercial

Sour dressing, non-butterfat, cultured, filled cream-type

Soy milk, fluid

Soy sauce made from soy and wheat (shoyu)

Soybeans, green, cooked, boiled, drained, without salt

Soybeans, mature cooked, boiled, without salt

Spaghetti w/Meat Sauce, frozen entree

Spaghetti, cooked, enriched, without added salt

Spaghetti, whole-wheat, cooked

Spices, celery seed

Spices, chili powder

Spices, cinnamon, ground

Spices, curry powder

Spices, garlic powder

Spices, onion powder

Spices, oregano, dried

Spices, paprika

Spices, parsley, dried

Spices, pepper, black

Common Measure	Content per Measure
1 cup	16.592
1 cup	10.175
1 cup	19.008
1 cup	11.978
1 tbsp	0.562
1 cup	11.368
1 tbsp	1.362
1 cup	19.890
1 cup	17.080
1 package	43.129
1 cup	39.676
1 cup	37.156
1 tsp	0.827
1 tsp	1.421
1 tsp	1.837
1 tsp	1.163
1 tsp	2.036
1 tsp	1.694
1 tsp	0.966
1 tsp	1.171
1 tbsp	0.672
1 tsp	1.361

Description

Spinach souffle, home-prepared

Spinach, canned, drained solids

Spinach, cooked, boiled, drained, without salt

Spinach, frozen, chopped or leaf, cooked, boiled, drained, without salt

Spinach, raw

Spinach, raw

Squash, summer, all varieties, cooked, boiled, drained, without salt

Squash, summer, all varieties, raw

Squash, winter, all varieties, cooked, baked, without salt

Squash, winter, butternut, frozen, cooked, boiled, without salt

Strawberries, frozen, sweetened, sliced

Strawberries, raw

Strawberries, raw

Strawberries, raw

Sugars, brown

Sugars, granulated

Sugars, powdered

Sweet rolls, cinnamon, commercially prepared with raisins

Sweet rolls, cinnamon, refrigerated dough with frosting, baked

Sweetpotato, canned, syrup pack, drained solids

Sweetpotato, canned, vacuum pack

Sweetpotato, cooked, baked in skin, without salt

Sweetpotato, cooked, boiled, without skin

Common Measure	Content per Measure
1 cup	2.829
1 cup	7.276
1 cup	6.750
1 cup	9.804
1 cup	1.089
1 leaf	0.363
1 cup	7.758
1 cup	3.786
1 cup	18.143
1 cup	24.120
1 cup	66.096
1 cup	12.749
1 strawberry	0.922
1 strawberry	1.382
1 tsp	3.115
1 tsp	4.199
1 tbsp	7.968
1 roll	30.540
1 roll	16.830
1 cup	49.706
1 cup	53.856
1 potato	30.237
1 potato	27.643

Description

Sweetpotato, cooked, candied, home-prepared

Syrups, chocolate, fudge-type

Syrups, corn, light

Syrups, maple

Syrups, table blends, pancake

Syrups, table blends, pancake, reduced-calorie

Taco shells, baked

Tangerine juice, canned, sweetened

Tangerines, (mandarin oranges), canned, light syrup pack

Tangerines, (mandarin oranges), raw

Tapioca, pearl, dry

Tea, brewed, prepared with tap water

Tea, herb, chamomile, brewed

Tea, herb, other than chamomile, brewed

Tea, instant, sweetened with sodium saccharin, lemon-flavored, prepared

Tea, instant, sweetened with sugar, lemon-flavored, without added ascorbic acid, powder, prepared

Tea, instant, unsweetened, powder, prepared

Toaster pastries, brown-sugar-cinnamon

Toaster pastries, fruit (includes apple, blueberry, cherry, strawberry)

Toaster Pastries, KELLOGG, KELLOGG'S POP TARTS, Frosted chocolate fudge

Tofu, firm, prepared with calcium sulfate and magnesium chloride (nigari)

Common Measure	Content per Measure
1 piece	29.253
1 tbsp	11.951
1 tbsp	15.926
1 tbsp	13.418
1 tbsp	12.294
1 tbsp	6.645
1 medium	8.299
1 cup	29.880
1 cup	40.799
1 tangerine	9.400
1 cup	134.809
6 fl oz	0.534
6 fl oz	0.356
6 fl oz	0.356
8 fl oz	1.043
8 fl oz	22.093
8 fl oz	0.403
1 pastry	34.050
1 pastry	36.972
1 pastry	37.336
1/4 block	2.406

Description

Tofu, soft, prepared with calcium sulfate and magnesium chloride (nigari)

Tomatillos, raw

Tomato juice, canned, with salt added

Tomato products, canned, paste, without salt added

Tomato products, canned, puree, without salt added

Tomato products, canned, sauce

Tomatoes, red, ripe, canned, stewed

Tomatoes, red, ripe, canned, whole, regular pack

Tomatoes, red, ripe, raw, year round average

Tomatoes, red, ripe, raw, year round average

Tomatoes, red, ripe, raw, year round average

Tomatoes, red, ripe, raw, year round average

Tomatoes, sun-dried

Tomatoes, sun-dried, packed in oil, drained

Tortillas, ready-to-bake or -fry, corn

Tortillas, ready-to-bake or -fry, flour

Tostada with guacamole

Turkey and gravy, frozen

Turkey patties, breaded, battered, fried

Turkey roast, boneless, frozen, seasoned, light and dark meat, roasted

Turkey, all classes, dark meat, cooked, roasted

Turkey, all classes, giblets, cooked, simmered, some giblet fat

Common Measure	Content per Measure
1 piece	2.160
1 medium	1.986
1 cup	10.303
1 cup	49.544
1 cup	22.450
1 cup	18.057
1 cup	15.785
1 cup	9.384
1 cup	7.056
1 cherry tomato	0.666
1 slice	0.784
1 tomato	4.822
1 piece	1.115
1 piece	0.700
1 tortilla	12.116
1 tortilla	17.792
1 tostada	16.012
5-oz package	6.546
1 patty	10.048
3 oz	2.611
3 oz	0.000
1 cup	1.160

Description

Turkey, all classes, light meat, cooked, roasted

Turkey, all classes, meat only, cooked, roasted

Turkey, all classes, neck, meat only, cooked, simmered

Turnip greens, cooked, boiled, drained, without salt

Turnip greens, frozen, cooked, boiled, drained, without salt

Turnips, cooked, boiled, drained, without salt

Vanilla extract

Veal, leg (top round), separable lean and fat, cooked, braised

Veal, rib, separable lean and fat, cooked, roasted

Vegetable juice cocktail, canned

Vegetable oil, canola

Vegetables, mixed, canned, drained solids

Vegetables, mixed, frozen, cooked, boiled, drained, without salt

Vinegar, cider

Waffles, plain, frozen, ready-to-heat, toasted (includes buttermilk)

Waffles, plain, prepared from recipe

Water, municipal

Waterchestnuts, chinese, canned, solids and liquids

Watermelon, raw

Watermelon, raw

Wheat flour, white, all-purpose, enriched, bleached

Wheat flour, white, all-purpose, self-rising, enriched

Wheat flour, white, bread, enriched

Common Measure	Content per Measure
3 oz	0.000
1 cup	0.000
1 neck	0.000
1 cup	6.278
1 cup	8.167
1 cup	7.894
1 tsp	0.531
3 oz	0.000
3 oz	0.000
1 cup	11.011
1 tbsp	0.000
1 cup	15.094
1 cup	23.824
1 tbsp	0.885
1 waffle	13.431
1 waffle	24.675
8 fl oz	0.000
1 cup	17.220
1 cup	11.476
1 wedge	21.593
1 cup	95.388
1 cup	92.775
1 cup	99.366

Description

Wheat flour, white, cake, enriched

Wheat flour, whole-grain

Wild rice, cooked

WORTHINGTON FOODS, MORNINGSTAR FARMS "Burger" Crumbles

WORTHINGTON FOODS, MORNINGSTAR FARMS BETTER'N BURGERS, frozen

Yogurt, fruit, low fat, 10 grams protein per 8 ounce

Yogurt, plain, low fat, 12 grams protein per 8 ounce

Yogurt, plain, skim milk, 13 grams protein per 8 ounce

Yogurt, plain, whole milk, 8 grams protein per 8 ounce

Common Measure	Content per Measure
1 cup	106.901
1 cup	87.084
1 cup	34.998
1 cup	6.622
1 patty	7.531
8-oz container	43.244
8-oz container	15.981
8-oz container	17.434
8-oz container	10.578

CHAPTER 14

MAKING IT EASIER

You don't have to prepare every low-carb recipe in your own kitchen. There are thousands of low-carb products now in the marketplace with as many as 200 new ones being introduced every month.

This list contains the top recommended products by the review team at Low Carb Luxury. If you haven't heard of them, they're America's leading low-carb consumer Web site, online since 1999. They have a panel of experts drawn from the best minds in the industry.

Low Carb Luxury's Product Spotlight lists hundreds of low-carb foods actually tested for taste, carbohydrate and other nutritional content, used in recipes wherever applicable.

Lora Ruffner, R.N., and her partner, Neil Beaty,

editors and owners of the Web site and *Low Carb Luxury* online magazine, head a 22-person review team that puts these products through their paces. They generously have compiled this list of some of those foods to help YOU launch and maintain your new low-carb lifestyle.

The reviews are not paid-for plugs for products by manufacturers, but hard-headed, tough examinations of products with YOUR best interests in mind. Only the best make their spotlight. They include many of the foods most people believe they cannot eat on a low-carb diet — bread and baked goods, pastas and pizzas, candy and confections, hot and cold cereals, jams, syrups, spreads and much more — all neatly grouped to make them easy to find. Here are some of those reviewed products and who makes them:

Low Carb Luxury's Top Product Recommendations:

Splenda Sweetener:
Comments: The accepted standard of artificial sweeteners for low-carb dieters.
Manufacturer: McNeil Nutritionals, LLC.

MiniCarb Chocolate Bars:
Comments: Contain no sugar alcohols.
Manufacturer: CarbSense.

ImiTaters:

Comments: Gourmet frozen potato substitute (whipped cauliflower) in three varieties.
Manufacturer: Heritage Foods.

ZeroCarborita Drink Mixes:

Comments: Make low-carb margaritas, pina coladas, hurricanes, mai tais and more.
Manufacturer: Zero Carb Products Inc.

Geraldine's Bodacious Cheese Straws:

Comments: Net carb count is only 4 grams for a generous 12-piece serving.
Manufacturer: Geraldine's Bodacious Foods.

Duke's Mayonnaise:

Comments: Truly sugar-free real mayonnaise with a long history.
Manufacturer: C.F. Sauer Company.

Home Bistro Low-Carb Frozen Meals:

Comments: Chef-prepared entrees and desserts.
Manufacturer: Home Bistro.

Heinz One-Carb Ketchup:

Comments: Rich and thick. Sweetened with Splenda.
Manufacturer: Heinz Foods.

Cheeters Low Carb Crackers:
Comments: In plain, garlic, onion, rye, sesame and sweet cinnamon (with Splenda).
Manufacturer: Cheeters Diet Treats.

DaVinci Gourmet Sugar-Free Syrups:
Comments: The best-tasting all-round zero-carb syrups. Sweetened with Splenda.
Manufacturer: DaVinci Gourmet.

Plain Good Crackers:
Comments: Deliciously thin crackers low in carbs; high in crunch.
Manufacturer: Low Carb Chef.

Steels Gourmet Rocky Mountain Ketchup:
Comments: A sweet-spicy blend with Splenda.
Manufacturer: Steel's Gourmet Foods.

Designer Protein Powders:
Comments: The only clinically tested whey protein available today. Low calorie, low carb.
Manufacturer: Next Nutrition.

Natural Ovens Carb-Conscious Breads:
Comments: Contain no preservatives or trans fats. Three net carbs per slice.
Manufacturer: Natural Ovens Bakery.

Mt. Olive Sugar-Free Pickles:

Comments: Sweetened with Splenda. Strips, sandwich stuffers, chips, gherkins and sweet relish.

Manufacturer: Mt. Olive Pickle Company.

MacNut Oil:

Comments: High in antioxidants, high smoke-point, long shelf life, great ratio of omega-3 to omega-6 fatty acids.

Manufacturer: MacNut Oil, Inc.

Bob's Red Mill Vital Wheat Gluten:

Comments: Gluten, the natural protein in wheat, is 75 percent protein. 6 net carbs per 1/4 cup.

Manufacturer: Bob's Red Mill Natural Foods.

Low Carb Chef Bake Mix:

Comments: A low-carb version of Bisquik, this is very handy in baking low-carb breads and more.

Manufacturer: Low Carb Chef.

Expert Foods Company's Thickeners:

Comments: An entire line of low/zero carb thickeners for cooking and baking. Includes ThickenThin, not/Sugar, not/Cereal and more.

Manufacturer: Expert Foods.

Just The Cheese Snacks:

Comments: No fillers. Snacks made with just cheese.

Manufacturer: Specialty Cheese Company.

Carb Countdown Milk:

Comments: In chocolate, whole, 2 percent and skim.

Manufacturer: Hood Dairy.

Keto Bread Machine Mixes:

Comments: Their cinnamon raisin is especially delicious. They rise high and are light.

Manufacturer: Keto Foods.

Erythritol Sweetener:

Comments: Non-volatile sugar alcohol, this sweetener comes in powdered, extra-fine granular, and regular granular.

Manufacturer: Low Carb Chef.

Gourmet Cheese Crackers:

Comments: Made from baked cheese. Varieties are aged Parmesan, sesame, garlic, Italian herb, caraway and onion poppyseed.

Manufacturer: Kitchen Table Bakers.

Their recommendations for where to buy these items? Many can be found in your local health-food, specialty or grocery store, but if you cannot locate them, they recommend the following Web sites for online ordering:

Low-Carb Connoisseur: www.low-carb.com

Low-Carb Dieter's Page: www.lowcarbdieters.com

CarbSmart: www.carbsmart.com

At Low Carb Luxury (www.lowcarbluxury.com) you'll find many other links to online sources for these and other products.

And that's only the tip of the iceberg. A quick Google search online, using the search words "low-carb food products" brought forth — are you ready for this? — a staggering 1,200,000 Web sites, many of them offering thousands of different low-carb foods, including substitutes for the carb-laden foods we need to avoid. The Internet is a wonderful warehouse for low-carbers, packed to the brim with delightful low-carb foods.

At just one Web site, www.lowcarbnexus.com, we found this extensive product list, complete with descriptions and prices, which are subject to change:

$5.99. Joe Bread Low Carb Bread (One 1 lb. [453 g] Loaf - Approx. 22 slices per bag).

$3.99. La Tiara. Low Carb Taco Shells (18 Shells, 4.3 oz. total).

$3.29. La Tortilla Factory Low Carb Tortillas (Package of 10 tortillas — Net Weight 13 oz. [368.6g]) La Tortilla Factory Low Carb Tortillas (also called wraps at Subway) are specially formulated to be both low-carb and low-fat! The new formulation includes Soy Protein and is a good source of protein and fiber. *The fiber count allows you to deduct the fiber count from the total carb count, giving the three active carb value per tortilla.

$5.99. Labrada Carbwatchers Gourmet Bread Mix (1 Bag) Gourmet Bread Mix allows you to bake your own thick, wholesome, delicious bread for you and your family. With only 3 grams of net-impact carbs per serving, and 0 grams of trans-fats.

$5.79. Labrada Carbwatchers Gourmet Dinner Roll Mix (1 Bag). Biscuits and rolls can now be served with dinner again! Carbwatchers Gourmet Dinner Roll Mix allows you to bake your own light, fluffy dinner rolls, with only 2 grams of net impact carbs per serving and 0 grams of trans fats!

$2.59. Nature's Own Reduced Carb Premium Wheat Bread (One 20 oz. [1 lb. 4 oz. - 567g] loaf - approx. 20 slices per bag), 5 grams of carbs per slice.

$2.49. O'SoLo Lo-Carb. Deli Rollz (One Box of 3 - 2.5 oz. Rollz) You get three big rolls per box, and each and every roll (both halves together) are as low as only 3.8 effective (impact) carbs (that's for the Original, the Onion is 5.2, and the Italian is 4.6!).

$2.59. O'SoLo Lo-Carb. Rollz (One Package of four 2 oz. Rollz), each roll containing only 3.1 effective carbs.

$5.99. Sinfully Lo-Carb Low Carbohydrate Pre-Sliced Bread (One 1 lb. [453g] Loaf - Approx. 16 slices per bag), with 3 grams per slice.

$3.29. Southern Signature Food's Mama Lupe's Low Carb Tortillas (Low Carb Wraps) - Package of 10 tortillas - 12.5 oz. [360g].

$2.69. Controlled Carb Gourmet Brownies (One 3 oz. [84.9g] brownie); only 1.5 carbs each.

$1.49. Carborite Creme Filled Cookies (One bag of three cookies [42g]).

$0.98. CARBORITE Individually Wrapped, Premium Cookies (One 1.1 oz. [30g] cookie), containing 1.7 effective carbs each.

$10.80. CARBORITE Individually Wrapped, Premium Cookies (One box of 12 - 1.1 oz. [30g] cookies).

$6.75. Low Carb Chef Low Carb Shortbread Cookies (One package of approx. 20 cookies - Approx. 100 grams).

$3.89. Low Carb Creations Sugar-Free Cookies (One package of 4 - 1 oz. cookies).

$5.49. Low Carb Enchantments Sugar-Free Cookies (One box of 6 - 1 oz. cookies).

$0.99. Southern Signature Food's Southern Delite Low Carb Cookies (One 1.13 oz. [32g.] cookie).

$23.75, Southern Signature Food's Southern Delite Low Carb Cookies (One Box of 25 individually wrapped 1.13 oz. [32g] Cookies). The flavors are: Lemon Zest (Lemon Almond), Chocolate Chip and Almond Brownie.

$6.50. CHEETERS Diet Treats Cinnamon Raisin Bread (One 1.24 lb. [568g] loaf - approx. 16 slices per bag).

$7.50. Cheeters Diet Treats Muffins (One Package of 6 muffins - 1.

$2.59. O'SoLo Lo-Carb. Sweet Rollz (One package of four 2 oz. Rollz), with 3.3 carbs each.

$4.49. Atkins Advantage 4-Pack of Low Carb Shakes (1 box of four - 325 ml cans) (Only two grams of impact carbs per Serving!) High in protein to keep your energy up; with calcium, 18 essential nutrients and absolutely no sugar added!

$3.99. Atkins Morning Start ZERO Carb Drink Mix - 1 canister - Each canister makes 32 - 8 oz. servings Morning Start Drink Mixes are sweetened with sucralose (Splenda brand) and they contain no artificial colors, flavors or preservatives! Each canister has four containers in it, and each container makes two quarts!

$14.99. Carborite Whey Protein Shake Mixes (One 14.7 oz. [418g] canister - approx. 11 servings).

$14.79. Doctor's Diet LowCarb Smoothies (One 1 lb. [454g] canister - approx. 15 servings).

$1.49. electroBlast Low Carb Beverage Twin Pack (Two Fizz-Tabs) Many people are deficient in the minerals that form electrolytes. Studies show that performance sports, exercise, dehydration and stress may contribute to electrolyte depletion. Modern food refining/processing operations and trace minerals depletion in soils used for crops may also contribute to our low trace minerals intake from food.

$6.59. Low Carb Keto Hot Cocoa (One 8.8 oz. [250g] can - approx 30 servings) Fights carb cravings! 30 servings. Only 2 grams of effective carbohydrates per serving!

$6.59. Keto Low Carb Milk (One 6.7 oz. [190g] can - approx. 11 servings) Keto Milk has delicious, creamy, whole milk taste and is a great alternative to cow's milk, which is very high in carbs due to milk sugars! Plus, Keto Milk is low in lactose ... with 90 percent less than regular milk! Add to that only 1 gram of carbs per cup ... and 8 grams of protein, and it comes in both regular and chocolate milk.

$15.99. Keto Shakes (One 17.5 oz. [495g]

canister - approx. 11 servings), 24 grams of protein per serving and 600mg of glutamine peptides fight carb and sweet cravings.

$5.99. Low Carb Creations Sipper Sweets Beverages (One 4 oz. [115g] Can - Approx. 46 servings) Instant low carb beverages! Just add water, and you have a refreshingly different low-carb, sugar-free drink! NO sugar ... NO saccharin ... NO Aspartame ... lemonade (1 Carb). Cappuccino (3 Carbs) Hot Cocoa (3 Carbs) Raspberry Lemon (1 Carb).

$1.29. Nexus Nutrition Stevi-Ade Zero Carb Drink Mix (One Canister - makes 2 quarts - approx. 8 servings), with 0 carbs.

$1.79. Z'LECTRA Sport Supplement Beverages (One 20 oz. bottle) contains 0 carbs.

$19.95. *A Complete Low Carb Lifestyle* (One hardback book) *An Executive Chef's Low Carb Lifestyle Culinary Guide.* This is a VERY exciting new book ... in fact, what we have are the very first release copies, making us among the first to have them in hand to offer to you! The author is Chef Gregory Pryor, C.E.C. Why are we so excited? Because Chef Pryor was a staff chef for the Atkins Group ... and has developed many exciting, luscious low-carb recipes that will knock your socks off!

$23.95. Atkins Answer Video Tape Set (Set of Two VHS format tapes) Dr. Robert C. Atkins, M.D., was the world's foremost expert on the controlled carbohydrate (low-carb) diet and lifestyle! In this special two video tape set, he personally teaches his dietary lifestyle and gives hints and tips on doing the diet! The set INCLUDES a FREE Basic Diet Manual Mini-Book as well! This series sells for $29.95 retail, but we have been able to make it available for $23.95!

$4.70. *Dr. Atkins NEW Carbohydrate Gram Counter Book* (One 128-page mini-book).

$7.5. *Dr. Atkins NEW Diet Revolution Book* (One paperback book).

$12.89. *Fabulous Lo-Carb Cuisine Cook Book* (One paperback book), by Ruth Glick.

$5.99. Atkins Morning Start Low Carb Breakfast Bars (One box of 5 - 1.4 oz. bars) Atkins Nutritionals.

$4.49. Carborite Low Carb Cereal Bars (One box of five 180g bars), with 4 or less impact carbs each.

$5.99. Atkins Morning Start Breakfast Cereals (One 10 oz. box), in the following flavors: Crunchy Almond Crisp, Banana Nut Harvest and Blueberry Bounty.

$6.95. Carbsense Mini-Carb Low-Carb Granola (One 11 oz. box), contains 4 impact carbs each.

$5.99. Keto Crisp Crispy Soy Cereal (One 8 oz. box) (Cocoa Crisp is slightly higher than the Keto Crisp); 2 carbs.

$15.51. Expert Foods Grits Extender (One Packet) Grits is a Southern favorite, a hot cereal made from hominy which is a kind of corn. Expert Foods Grits Mix is an extender to stretch a little bit of the real thing into a portion large enough to satisfy. Please note: this product is for use as a cereal only. It does not harden on cooling, which makes it unsuitable for fried grits. However, it does make a delicious side dish, a la mashed potatoes, especially with cheese.

$15.51. Expert Foods ThickenThin not/Cereal Thickener (One 5 oz. packet - 22 servings) ThickenThin not/Cereal thickener is an unflavored mix that gives you the thick, creamy texture of hot cereal, rather like cream of wheat or rice.

$4.99. Gram's Gourmet Cream of Flax Hot Cereals - 14 oz. bag, with 3 grams of net carbs per serving.

$6.49. Keto Low Carb Hot Cereals (One 12.5 oz. canister - 9 servings); 3g effective carbs, 17g protein and 9g fiber! 12.5 oz. - 9 servings.

$7.69. Flax-O-Meal Low Carb Hot Cereal (One 12 oz. bag - approx. 10 servings). Rich in healthy flax seed meal, each serving has less than 2 digestible carbs, 16g of protein and a whopping 10g of dietary fiber! Available in these flavors: Cinnamon Spice, Vanilla Almond , Butter Pecan, Strawberry Cream. Simply mix with hot water and stir it up ... smell the delicious aroma and then ...

$7.49. Carbsense Pancake & Waffle Mix (One 12 oz. box - approx. 8 servings), 2 grams of effective carbs per pancake.

$8.99 Ketogenics Low Carb Pancake Mix (One 16 oz. box - approx. 10 servings).

$3.89. Atkins Sugar-Free Pancake Syrup (One 12 oz. bottle). Sugar-free, zero carb pancake syrup!

$4.19. Allen Wertz Simply Sugar Free. Candies (One 5 oz. bag - approx. 5 servings) ... smooth, chocolate-y and totally sugar-free and low carb!

$1.99. CARBOLITE Chocolate Bars (One 1.75 oz. bar) These bars are incredible! Enjoy rich, dark, semi-sweet chocolate, or rich milk chocolate, milk chocolate with almonds, chocolate crisp and NOW... they have white chocolate crisp and white with almonds!

$45.40. CARBOLITE Chocolate Bars (One box of 24 - 1.75. oz. bars) These bars are incredible!

$1.49. Gol D Lite Disco Nuts Low Carb Candies (One bag - 1.76 oz. [50g]), 1.6 net carbs per serving.

$1.49. Gol D Lite Zero's Low Carb Candies (One bag - 1.76 oz. [50g]), 2.3 net carbs per serving!

$1.79. Pure De-lite Chocolate Bars (One 1.33 oz. [38g] bar).

$37.95. Pure De-lite Chocolate Bars (One BOX of 24 1.33 oz. [38g] bars). These are the real Belgian chocolate bars that you have heard so much about.

$2.99. Pure De-lite Dip & Twist Chocolate Covered Pretzels (One 2 oz. bag). Each 2 oz. bag is under 4 effective grams of carbohydrate. Pure De-lite Chocolate Covered Pretzels Carb Count Pure De-lite Milk Chocolate 4 grams per 2 oz. bag. Pure De-lite Dark Chocolate 3 grams.

$7.99. Russell Stover Low Carb Assorted Candies (One box [8.25 oz.] of 18 assorted candies), 0.3 of a gram of impact carbs for the candies in this sampler.

$7.99. Russell Stover Low Carb Whitman Sampler Assorted Candies (One box [7 oz.] of 15 assorted candies).

$1.79. Gol D Lite Sugar-Free Chews (One 1.76 oz. [50g] bag) zero carbs!

$5.49.   Judy's   Sugar-Free   Assorted

Caramels (One 1.76 oz. [50g] bag) ... available in assorted flavors ... Vanilla Caramels, Vanilla Almond, Triple Treat and Assorted.

$1.59. Pure De-Lite Chewy Sensations (One 1.1 oz. bar); Pure De-lite Chewy Sensations Carb Count Pure De-lite Milk Chocolate Mocha 4.2 grams per bar. Pure De-lite Dark Chocolate Mint 3 grams per bar. Pure De-lite Dark Chocolate Licorice 3 grams.

$52.25. Pure De-Lite Chewy Sensations (One box of 36 1.1 oz. Bars). Each bar under 5 effective grams of carbohydrate ; here's how they break down: Pure De-lite Chewy Sensations Carb Count Pure De-lite Milk Chocolate Mocha 4.2 grams per bar Pure De-lite Dark Chocolate Mint 3 grams per bar.

$2.99. CARBOLITE Chocolate Covered Almonds (One 1.77 oz. [50g] bag) .3 grams of carbs per almond.

$5.89. Keto Nuts (One 4 oz. jar) Keto Nuts are sugar-free, Aspartame-free & saccharin free! They also come in at 1 gram ECC* per serving (1 oz.)! Sweetened with Splenda.

$1.29. Megan's Low Carb Orange Spice

Candied Pecans (1 - 2 oz. package) (Only two grams of impact carbs per serving!) Megan's Low Carb Orange Spice Candied Pecans are handmade in a Seattle kitchen from an old family recipe! They are delicious on salads and in stir-fry, or in a cookie dough mix. Better yet, they are a wonderful snack all by themselves!

$2.29. CARBOLITE Jelly Based Candies (One 3 oz. [85g] bag) These are fun, tasty candies!!! Now you can have Jelly Beans just like you used to! And, if you are into sour candies, the Sour Citrus are eye-poppers! These candies are sugar-free and almost zero carbs! (The Sour Citrus is only .4 of 1 carb per piece (or 6 carbs for 15 pieces), and the Jelly Beans are .115 of one carb per piece (or 3 carbs for 26 Jelly Beans).

$1.79. Gol D Lite Rainbow Salad Hard Fruit Candy (One 1.76 oz. bag) with 0 carbs.

$3.59. Heavenly Desserts Meringues (One 1.6 oz. box - approx. 30 pieces) Sugar-free, fat-free and sweetened with Splenda. No calories, no cholesterol, no sodium ... totally guilt-free!

$2.99. Judy's Sugar-Free, Low Carb Brittles (One 4 oz. round) (The Mixed Nut is slightly higher in price.) These sugar-free, low-carb brittles are the most popular thing to arrive at the Low Carb Nexus Store in a LONG time.

$5.49. Judy's Sugar-Free, Low Carb Brittles (One 8 oz. rectangle).

$1.69. Blitz Power Mints (One 50 mint canister) These intense mints from Great Britain freshen your breath and leave a pleasant taste in your mouth, and they come in a handy pocket dispenser. Most sugar-free mints in the stores are STILL up to one carb per mint ... these are ZERO net carbs per TWO mints! There are 50 mints in each pocket dispenser! NOTE: These mints are sweetened with Splenda.

$1.29. Atkins Endulge Candies (One package of 3 - 1.2 oz. cups) Dr. Atkins' labs have come up with some great candies!

$17.95. Atkins Endulge Candies (One box of 15 packages of 3 - 1.2 oz. cups).

$1.29. Atkins Endulge Wafer Crisps (One 1 oz. package - 2 bars) ... sugar-free and low-carb! There are two crisps in each package ... the whole package is just FOUR IMPACT CARBS!

$17.95. Atkins Endulge Wafer Crisps (One box of 15 - 1 oz. - 2 bar packages).

$2.59. Carb Slim Bites (One 1. 5 oz. box) ... Zero sugar carbs and, after deducting dietary fiber and polyols, they are ZERO impact carbs per serving!

$29.88. Carb Slim Bites (One case of 12 - 1.5 oz. boxes).

$1.39. CARBOLITE Low Carb Snack Bars - Caramel (One 1 oz. bar).

$20.65. CARBOLITE. Low Carb Snack Bars - Caramel Bar (Box of 16 1 oz. bars). CARBOLITE has somehow managed to closely match the taste of some very well-known chocolate snack bars ... the Caramel Nougat bar tastes just like a Milky Way.

$1.39. CARBOLITE Low Carb Snack Bars - Caramel Nougat (One 1.1 oz. bar).

$15.50. CARBOLITE Low Carb Snack Bars - Caramel Nougat (Box of 12 - 1.1 oz. bars).

$1.39. CARBOLITE Low Carb Snack Bars - Crispy Caramel (One 1.1 oz. bar).

$15.50. CARBOLITE Low Carb Snack Bars - Crispy Caramel (Box of 12 - 1.1 oz. Bars).

$1.39. CARBOLITE Low Carb Snack Bars - Peanut Butter Cup (One 1.2 oz. cup).

$15.50. CARBOLITE Low Carb Snack Bars - Peanut Butter Cup (Box of 12 - 1.2 oz. bars).

$1.39. CARBOLITE Low Carb Snack Bars - Peanut Caramel Nougat (One 1.1 oz. bar).

$15.50. CARBOLITE Low Carb Snack Bars - Peanut Caramel Nougat (Box of 12 - 1.1 oz. bars).

$1.39. CARBOLITE Low Carb Snack Bars - Pecan Cluster Bar (One 1 oz. bar).

$20.65. CARBOLITE Low Carb Snack Bars - Pecan Cluster (Box of 16 - 1 oz. bars).

$1.39. CARBOLITE Low Carb Snack Bars - Toffee (One 1 oz. bar).

$20.65. CARBOLITE Low Carb Snack Bars - Toffee (Box of 16 - 1 oz. bars).

$1.49. Gol D Lite Brand Lite Rafts (One 1.5 oz. bag - 4 pieces per pack) These Lite Rafts are a very thin layer of cookie-like (sort of like a Kit Kit) material, then a thin layer of white cream, then a layer of chocolate ... all wrapped in neat gold foil! Strange, unique, but tasty! And at only one-half of one impact carb per piece.

$1.79. Gol D Lite Mousse Pillows (One bag of 2 - 1.4 oz. pieces).

One note: These new products have labeling that conforms to the new FDA standards. The FDA is requiring all manufacturers to put the FULL carb count on each label.

$0.89. La Nouba Silhouette Chocolate Cream Candies (One 0.64 oz. [18g] bar) La Nouba Candies are soft, creamy and dreamy! They are very low carb, with just 1.44 grams of effective carbs per piece (depending on flavor). They are sugar-free, all natural and only 72 calories apiece! They are fortified with calcium and magnesium to be a healthy snack as well! And though they are very low carb, they also contain 30 percent less fat than regular chocolate!

$0.79. Pure De-lite Chocolate Truffles (One 0.43 oz. individual truffle). Pure De-lite Truffles have no waxes, no artificial flavors and no preservatives! Each truffle is 0.43 ounces, or 12 grams.

$48.30. Pure De-lite Chocolate Truffles (One box of 70 0.43 oz. truffles).

$1.49. Pure De-lite Caramel Candy Snack Bars (One 1 oz. bar).

$22.25. Pure De-lite Caramel Candy Snack Bars (One box of 16 - 1 oz. bars). Each bar is under 2 effective grams of carbohydrate.

$2.99. Russell Stover Bag of Low Carb Candies (One 3.5 oz. bag - approx. 12 pieces). At 0.2 of a gram of impact carbs for the truffle cups, 0.5 of a gram of impact carbs for the Peanut Butter Cups and 0.8 of a gram of an impact carb for the Pecan Delights ... these candies are very LOW in carbs, while being BIG on taste!

$4.99. Russell Stover Box of Low Carb Candies (One Box of Approx. 20 - 6 oz. pieces). At 0.2 of a gram of Impact Carbs for the Milk Chocolate with Almonds, the Solid Milk Chocolate and the French Mint Candies ... these candies are very LOW in Carbs.

$1.29. Russell Stover Two Pack of Low Carb Candies (One 1 oz. package of two candies). Only 0.1 of a gram of impact carbs for the

Mint Patties, 0.2 of a gram of impact carbs for the Toffee Squares and 1.2 impact carbs for the Pecan Delights.

$3.99. Colac Pie Fillings Colac Pie Fillings are awesome! And at ONLY 1 gram of impact carbs per serving ... it is also VERY low carb!

$1.69. Eden Organic Black Soybeans (One 15 oz. can) Eden Black Soybeans are delicious, highly versatile and exceptionally nutritious. They're ideal in salads, casseroles and with low-carb pasta! Many low-carb recipes call for this specific brand of black soybeans!

$16.99. ThickenThin not/Starch (One packet) The perfect thickener for low carb or grain-free diets. not/Starch recreates the thick rich textures you want without adding calories, fat or carbohydrates. It even gives you fiber, all of it the soluble fiber that is so hard to get on a restricted diet. (Note: Expert Foods follows U.S. nutrition label law which requires reporting 4 calories per gram from soluble fiber, even though the human body cannot digest it.)

$13.99. ThickenThin not/Sugar (One 6.75 oz. packet) Formulated to give the texturizing effect of sugar in beverage and syrup recipes even on low-carb or other sugar-free diets. not/Sugar is unsweetened to allow you to select the sweeteners of your choice. Add the sweetener of your choice and recreate the rich-mouth feel of sugar-sweetened beverages — stretch small amounts of fruit and/or dairy into big satisfying shakes!

$4.49. Expert Foods' Wise CHOice Cake-ability Baking Aid (1 - 6 oz. package) (One package is enough for three 1.5 pound cakes or tea breads.) Expert Foods' Wise CHOice Cake-ability Baking Aid is the perfect way to turn ground nuts and nut flours into delicious, moist baked goods that taste and feel the way cakes and muffins should!

$9.99. Expert Foods RealCream (One packet) Here's a special treat for coffee-lover s... honest-to-goodness dried dairy cream for your coffee, even when you are away from refrigeration! Now you don't have to do without — why settle for the synthetic stuff? Dried cream is slightly higher in carbs than liquid heavy cream (cream is basically fat, so it has to be dried on something else — in this case nonfat milk), but RealCream has only one-fourth the carbs of commercial non-dairy creamers.

$5.79. Gringo Billy's Low Carb Chili Mix (One 4 oz. bag - approx. 14 servings) Gringo Billy has a unique sense of humor! His label tells us that his Gourmet Spices are so fresh you should slap 'em! Cute! But his product is very good! Very tasty and very low carb! After subtracting for fiber, how about zero impact carbs? Yep! This will make one powerful chili ... try using our Eden Black Soybeans with this mix! You can't go wrong! No MSG, no added sugar.

$2.79. Gringo Billy's Low Carb Guacamole Mix (One 0.63 oz. packet - approx. 8 servings).

$1.29. Gringo Billy's Low Carb Taco Seasoning (One 0.91 oz. bag - approx. 11 servings). After subtracting for fiber, how about 0.2 (less than 1) impact carbs? No MSG, no added sugar.

$3.29. Guiltless Gourmet Low Carb Bean Dips (1 - 16 oz. [453g] jar) These low carb bean Dips are tasty and the spicy one is, well, SPICY! Try them with our R.W. Garcia's Lo Carb Tortilla Chips! Only 4 grams of net carbs for the Mild, and 3 grams of net carbs for the Spicy flavor.

$3.99. Keto Crumbs (One 11.6 oz. can) Now

you can enjoy crispy, crunchy fried chicken, fish, shrimp, pie crusts and much, much more ... without all the carbs! With just 4 grams of carbs in each ounce (enough to coat 4 6-ounce pieces of chicken), Keto Crumbs are a real low-carb bargain; especially when you consider typical high-carb breadings contain 20 grams of carbs per ounce! Plus Keto Crumbs are higher in protein than all other crumb coatings.

$1.00. Low Carb Depot Accu-Carb Breadcrumbs (1 - 6 oz. tub) (1 gram of impact carbs per serving!) Accu-Carb has "a carb count you can count on!" Their low-carb, high-protein, sugar-free breadcrumbs are also bromate-free! With only ONE effective impact carb per serving.

$12.99. Nexus Nutrition PureProteam Egg White Protein (One 1 lb. bag). Yes, this product may seem a little higher than our other bake mix ingredients, but you DO have to break a lot of eggs to produce this much pure egg white protein! And, since it is pure, with no fillers, or flavorings added, it is zero carb! Now you can add pure egg white protein to your own recipes, shakes, ice creams, whatever your creative mind can develop! Pure, natural, egg white protein also has no cholesterol or fat!

$4.99. Nexus Nutrition PureProteam Soy Protein Isolate (One 1 lb. bag - approx. 16 servings). Many low-carb recipes call for pure soy protein isolate, but that can be very hard to find! Soy Protein Isolate has been garnering lots of attention lately due to its health benefits for your heart. This is plain, unflavored Soy Protein Isolate and is appropriate for use in bake mixes, as a thickener, and can even be used to make healthy high-protein beverages!

$7.99. Nexus Nutrition PureProteam Whey Protein (One 10 oz. bag - approx. 5 servings). Dr. Atkins says in his book, *Dr. Atkins New Diet Revolution*, that whey protein is the best type to use! Use this as a bake mix additive in your own recipes, shakes, ice creams.

$2.19. Rosie's Gold Low Carb Sloppy Joe Sauce (1 - 8.45 oz. Jar) (Only four grams of impact carbs per serving!) Rosie's Gold Sloppy Joe Sauce gives you a low-carb alternative to make an old favorite! Low fat, zero trans fats and ZERO cholesterol as well!

$2.50. Steel's Low Carb, Sugar-Free Dressings and Sauces (1 bottle) Less than one or two grams of carbs per serving (depending on flavor) Steel's Dressings and Sauces are made sugar-free and extremely low-carb! They are sweetened with Splenda and make great additions to your cooking and marinade options!

$4.49. Sugarless Confectionery Chocolate Chips (One half-pound bag) Using our Bake*Lite Reduced Carb Flour, and these great low-carb chocolate chips, you can have those low-carb cookies ... fresh out of the oven! And they are only 4 carbs per 1/2 cup.

$2.49. Atkins Crunchers Low Carb Snack Chips (One 1 oz. bag); approximately 4 grams per bag of chips (effective carbs) depending on flavor.

$2.99. Carbsense Aramana Soy Pretzels (One 3 oz. bag) These are great, new pretzels! They are not your typical pretzel taste — more like a mild, crunchy cheese flavor — but it is awesome! We all know the benefits of soy for your health and these have 10 grams of soy protein available! They are all natural, low in fat as well ... in short, a great healthy snack! These pretzels are hearth baked and only 8 grams of impact carbohydrates per serving.

$3.69. Carbsense Soy Multi-Grain Tortilla Chips (One 5.5 oz. bag - approx. 5 servings.)

$1.59. Hain Celestials Carb Fit Twirls Low Carb Soy Snack (1 oz. bag) An all-natural soy snack for the low carb lifestyle, with 5g of net carbs per serving.

$2.89. Just the Cheese Crunchy Baked Cheese (One 2 oz. bag) 100 percent natural cheese for 100 percent cheese taste. The good folks in Wisconsin have found a 17-step baking process that makes natural cheese into a crunchy snack! Since there are very few carbohydrates in cheese, their new baked cheeses are an ideal addition to a low carbohydrate diet! To make them, they simply take slices of their natural cheeses, season and then gently bake them to crisp, delicious perfection. Nothing else is added.

$3.25. R.W. Garcia's Lo Carb Tortilla Chips (1 - 10 oz. [283g] bag). They're really low carb! Only 9 grams of net carbs (after deducting the 5 grams of dietary fiber per serving).

$1.69. Betafoods Chip's Chips CheeseThins (One 1 oz. [28g] bag). True low carb - high protein snack that can be munched on all day, everyday! With zero grams of total carbs and 16 grams of protein, amazingly totally zero carb!

$1.69. Betafoods Chip's Chips Snackers

(One 1 oz. [28g] bag), with only 2 grams of total carbs and 16 grams of protein.

$2.59. Blue Diamond NutThins. (One 4.5 oz. box - approx. 64 wafers) Blue Diamond NutThins are delicious, nutritious gourmet snack crackers. They are light, crispy wafers made from natural California rice and rich, flavorful nuts. No wheat gluten is added. They are 1.3 grams of carbohydrate per NutThin so they are NOT necessarily for induction phase dieting! However, if you are on Ongoing Weight Loss or Maintenance Phase, these are all natural, crisp crackers with an EXCELLENT taste!

$4.99. Cheeters Diet Treats Low Carb Crackers (One 4 oz. box) These very low-carb crackers are 1/3 of one gram of a carbohydrate per one whole cracker. In other words, three crackers are only one gram of carbs. And, they are each about the size of a regular graham cracker! Flavors: Plain. Cinnamon.

$3.25. FiberRich 100% Natural Wheat Bran Fiber Crackers (One 4.4 oz. box) You loved the Bran-A-Crisp Wheat Bran Fiber Bread we used to carry, but now it is no longer available. However, FiberRich Bran Bread has the same great taste ... and at a better price! It looks and tastes just like Bran-A-Crisp and is a crispy cracker-like, high-fiber product. It is imported from Norway! It has 12 grams of carbs and 5 grams of fiber ... per TWO crackers ... that is a net value of 3.5 grams of effective carbs.

$5.45. Low Carb Chef Plain Good Crackers (One bag). These are, as the name suggests, just... Plain Good! That is, they are simple, crunchy, thin crackers that are EXCEL-LENT with a good, low-carb cheese topping! Man!!! Put a little cheese on these and they are wonderful! And as a snack they are great by themselves as well!

$2.99. Gram's Gourmet Sweet Cinnamon & Butter & Cheddar Cheese Crunchies Pork Rinds (One 4 oz. bag) After losing 100 pounds on a low-carb diet, Julee, the founder of Gram's Gourmet, decided it was high time to take some of her recipes to market!

$1.20. Lowrey's Bacon Curls Microwave Pork Rinds (One 1.75 oz. bag). Pork rinds are ... pork rinds, right? Nope! Lowrey's has come up with a neat twist to an old standby! What would happen if you put pork rinds in a microwave and popped them up like popcorn? The result would be hot, crisp and light ... not cold and hard like store bought pork rinds! Hot, light, tasty ... and ZERO CARBS!!!

$4.99. Maisie Jane's Sliced Almond Delights (One bag - 4 oz.) Almonds are naturally low-carb ... but plain almonds can be, well, plain! So Maisie Jane has added some flavoring to spice them up.

$1.99. Pumpkorn Alternative Snack Food (One 2.75 oz. bag) Pumpkorn is an alternative to the typical snack! Low-carb and good tasting, this great snack food has been extolled by many, including Dr. Atkins, as an appropriate snack food for low-carb dieters.

$2.99. Belinda's Low Carb Kitchen Nuts (One 2 oz. bag). They come in two flavors: Cinnamon Praline Pecans and Cinnamon Praline Almonds! And the effective carb count is only 4 grams effective carbs (after deducting fiber).

$4.99. Gram's Flax 'n Nut Crunchies.

$1.79. Lean Protein Bites (One 1 oz. tube) Breakthrough Nutrition Lean Protein Bites are tasty, crunchy bites of flavor that are perfect for dropping in your pocket for a handy snacks.

Only ONE gram of carbohydrates per TUBE (except Vanilla, which is only 2 grams).

$19.99. Lean Protein Bites (One box of 12 1 oz. tubes.)

$6.95. Low Carb Success Flax-O-Meal Granola (One 9 oz. packet). With one effective carb after subtracting fiber and sugar alcohols, and 5 grams of protein, this is a sweet, crunchy, tasty treat that won't kill your ketosis!

$7.69. Low Carb Success Sweet Nut'Ns (One 6 oz. Packet) Imagine tasty low-carb nuts, coated with sweet, sugar-free coating ... and you have Sweet Nut'Ns! Made with ThickenThin not/Sugar (another low -carb product) and our old friend Splenda. Only TWO impact carbs per serving!

$4.99. Atkins Quick & Easy Fudge Brownie Mix (One 8.5 oz. packet - makes approx. 11 - 2 brownies). At 9 grams per 2-inch brownie, you can occasionally even allow yourself one if you are severely restricting your carb intake.

$6.99. Low Carb Chef Fudge Brownie Mix (One 12 oz. packet - makes approx. 9 - 2.5 brownies).

$7.99. Expert Foods Wise CHOice Cheesecake (One 1.75 oz. packet). Expert Foods is one of the pioneers in the low-carb foods industry ... and they KNOW their stuff! They have developed excellent desserts that have 4 grams of carbs and 4 grams of fiber ... for an ECC (effective carb count) of ZERO!

$9.49. Expert Foods Wise CHOice Frozen Dessert Mix (One 2 oz. packet) 4 grams of fiber ... for an ECC of ZERO!

$8.69. Expert Foods Wise CHOice Fudge Bar Mix (One 1.9 oz. packet); also 4 grams of carbs, and 4 grams of fiber ... for an ECC of ZERO!

$19.95. Expert Foods Wise CHOice Mousse Mix (One 6.5 oz. packet).

$4.99. Atkins Quick Quisine Muffin Mixes (One approx. 9 oz. bag) Hot, tasty muffins, right out of the oven! Oh, yeah! Now we're talkin'! These muffins are really good and they are low-carb! They come in at 2 to 8 grams of carbs per muffin (depending on flavor).

$6.99. Ketogenics Muffin Mixes (One approx. 13.5 oz. box). These great Ketogenics

Muffin Mixes are super low-carb — how about only ONE GRAM of impact carbs for the Chocolate Chip flavor and only TWO GRAMS for the Apple Cinnamon and TWO AND A HALF GRAMS for the yummy Wild Blueberry flavor! The fruit flavors have little cans inside with REAL FRUIT! These muffins are great tasting without sacrificing the low-carb lifestyle! And simple to make! All you will need is a few eggs, some oil and water.

$5.79. Labrada Nutrition CarbWatchers. Gourmet Cake & Muffin Mix (1 bag). Cakes and muffins have always been considered fattening, high-carb and a major no-no for the low-carb dieter. Not anymore! New Carbwatchers Gourmet Cake & Muffin Mix lets you bake delicious desserts and treats that are compatible with your carb-restricted diet. Each succulent serving contains only 3 grams of net-impact carbs, ZERO trans fats and a rich, delicious taste you'll love!

$8.49. Carbsense Zero Carb Baking Mix (One 14 oz. box). Unlike most low-carb baking mixes, Carbsense Zero Carb Baking Mix is a blend of soy protein isolates, oat bran, wheat protein and a pinch of baking soda. The result?

A ZERO carb baking mix you can use one-to-one as a replacement for flour!

$15.99. Fran Gare's Decadent Desserts Bake Mix (1 - 12 oz. [340g] can). This great bake mix is sugar-free, grain-free, gluten-free and low carbohydrate! Each can makes 2 to 4 desserts, and the recipes are right on the can! We have them at a special introductory price ... they are normally $15.99 and we have them for $13.99! They come in Chocolate and Almond flavors.

$5.95. Atkins Bread Mixes (One 12.6 oz. box).

$4.99. Atkins Corn Bread Muffin Mix (One 8.5 oz. packet). At 8 grams of effective carbs per muffin, you can even occasionally allow yourself one if you are severely restricting your carb intake (just be sure to count it)!

$5.95. Ketogenics Low Carb Bread Machine Mix (One 11.8 oz. box). Ketogenics, Inc. Low Carb Bread Machine Mix is the first low-carbohydrate yeast-risen bread machine mix on the market. And now, there are three great types of breads available: Original, Pumpernickel Rye and Honey Wheat!

$7.51. Low Carb Nexus Raw Macadamia Nut Flour (One 1 lb. bag).

$7.51. Low Carb Nexus Raw Almond Nut Flour (One 1 lb. bag).

$4.99. Low Carb Nexus Raw Brazil Nut Flour (One 1 lb. bag).

$7.51. Low Carb Nexus Raw Coconut Flour (One 1 lb. bag).

$7.50. Low Carb Nexus Raw Pecan Flour (One 1 lb. bag).

$5.99. Bake*Lite Reduced Carb Flour (One 1 lb. bag).

$5.99. Bake*Lite Whole Wheat Flour (One 1 lb. bag).

$5.99. Bake*lite Xtreme! Low Carb Flour (One 1 lb. bag).

$25.88. Low Carb Nexus Cholesterol Support (90 tablets) Helps support normal healthy cholesterol levels. America, in general, is getting panicky about their cholesterol levels! Fortunately, nature provides us with natural plant sterols as an easy way to help us manage our cholesterol levels! Cholestatin is a product of Degussa Bioactives ... a proprietary formulation of natural plant sterols.

$8.19. Low Carb Nexus Chromium (100 capsules) Yeast-free - 200 mcg. Chromium is a potent, bioactive source of the essential mineral chromium. It plays a vital role in sensitizing the body's tissues to the hormone insulin, performing these three major roles: The regulation of fat metabolism, the regulation of glucose metabolism, and the regulation of amino acid (protein) metabolism. ChromeMate brand of chromium has been shown to help to control appetite, especially sugar cravings!

$11.95. Low Carb Nexus Complete Essential Fatty Acids (60 capsules). Hexane free softgels essential fatty acids are the so-called good fats that have, for the most part, been excluded (until recently) from our foods by companies trying to produce products that are low-fat. Yet EFAs are vital to our health! As structural components of membranes, EFAs help form a barrier that keeps foreign molecules, viruses, yeasts, fungi and bacteria outside of cells.

$6.88. Low Carb Nexus Fiber Clean

Psyllium Husks (100 capsules). (*Plantago ovata*) - 500 mg. You may have noticed that if you don't eat your daily salad on your low-carb diet, you can get constipated! Not to worry — there is a natural alternative to harsh chemical laxatives, something healthy, gentle and natural, and recommended by low-carb experts like Dr. Atkins! The ingredient they mention? Psyllium!

$24.99. Low Carb Nexus Grape Seed Extract (90 capsules). You've heard that vitamins C, E and beta-carotene are potent antioxidants for good health. Grape Seed Extract is a far more powerful antioxidant.

$15.69. Low Carb Nexus Immune System Support (60 capsules). Our Low Carb Nexus Immune System Support is designed to support the body's immune system and help your body do what it was designed to do — stay healthy and vigorous! We start with the vitamins A, C, B-6, as well as folic acid, vitamin B-12, pantothenic acid and zinc, which are all important nutrients that support the immune system naturally.

$29.19. Low Carb Nexus L-Carnitine (60 tablets) 500 mg - with 10 mg vitamin B-6 per tablet. What if there were a nutrient that helped increase your energy, aided your weight loss efforts, increased your immune function and helped enhance your mental faculties — plus, lowered your cholesterol and triglycerides? Wouldn't it be wonderful? Well, it does exist! It is called L-Carnitine! L-Carnitine is a vitamin-like nutrient that provides all the above-mentioned benefits, and much more!

$20.48. Low Carb Nexus L-Glutamine (200 tablets) 500 mg. L-Glutamine has been shown to fight all kinds of cravings and benefit the immune system as well. A natural amino acid, L-Glutamine supplementation is safe and effective. Use L-Glutamine to help fight those sugar and carbohydrate cravings! As a naturally occurring amino acid, L-Glutamine is an important element in supplying the brain with energy.

$20.95. Low Carb Nexus Life Essentials Multi-Vitamin (90 tablets) Multi-vitamin and mineral with whole food concentrate. This is the first of our new line of vitamins and supplements we are recommending specifically for the low-carb lifestyle!

$6.25. Low Carb Nexus Pau d' Arco - 100 500mg capsules. A Candida fighting herb! Lapacho, a tree found in the dense rain forests of South America, is often used to make beautiful, fine-grained furniture. However, the inner bark of the Lapacho tree has other uses as well! Pau d'arco, an herb derived from the lapacho bark, is used frequently by many herbalists to treat fungal, bacterial and many parasitic infections.

$4.75. Low Carb Nexus Potassium - 100 tablets. Amino acid complex - 99 mg. Potassium is a mineral that works, in conjunction with with sodium, to regulate proper electrolyte balance and contributes to heart muscle health. It aids in changing glycogen to glucose, and helps to promote healing. Potassium can also be used to treat stress, diabetes, hypertension, hypoglycemia, water balance and distribution in the body, as well as muscle and nerve cell function, and kidney and adrenal function.

$24.40. SPECIAL DEAL! Our Low Carb Nexus Ultra-VMT Multi-Vitamin contains ALL the essential vitamins you need to begin your low-carb lifestyle, and it is now 25 percent off for a limited time! Why? Well, we want to introduce you to our excellent vitamins and supplements, specifically formulated for low-carb dieters!

$29.95. Low Carb Nexus Tonalin CLA (90 Capsules) Conjugated Linoleic AcidTonalin CLA is derived naturally from sunflower oil.

Clinical studies show that CLA works three ways to help you achieve your diet goals: CLA interferes with a substance in your body called lipoprotein lipase that helps store fat in your body. CLA helps your body use its existing fat for energy and increases lean muscle tissue, which naturally slims your body.

$2.69. Nature's Gate All-Natural, Sugar-Free ZAP Breath Strips. Breath Strips are low-carb! Maybe, but they still use sugar as their sweetener! These strips use Stevia Extract! They contain no sugar! And that is not the only benefit! ZAP controls bad breath with natural, herbal peppermint! It also contains Green Tea Extract, which is not only rich in antioxidants and is reported to help inhibit bacterial growth, it also helps burn fat!

$4.99. Atkins Quick Quisine Pasta Sides (One 4.7 oz. bag). These long-awaited pastas from Atkins Nutritionals are finally here! And they have proven themselves well worth the wait! These Pasta Sides come in three great varieties: Fettuccine, Alfredo, Elbow.

$5.99. Atkins Quick Quisine Spaghetti (1 box - 12 oz.). Now you can add your favorite pasta to your menu! Atkins Quick Quisine

Spaghetti, with 5 grams of net carbs per serving, is ready in less than 10 minutes! No trans fats; 5 net carbs per serving; no added sugars. Excellent source of fiber.

$1.79. Bella Vita Low Carb Pasta. Bella Vita low-carb pasta (imported from Italy) has 80 percent less carbs than regular pasta and is all natural, high protein and high fiber. With only 10 net carbs per serving it contains healthy soy protein (6.5 g per serving), and is cholesterol and GMO free!

$5.79. Carbsense Low Carb Garlic & Herb Pizza Crust Mix (One 12 oz. box). The herb & garlic taste is mild and adds to the overall taste of the pizza! Ingredients: vital wheat gluten, soy protein concentrate, oat fiber, wheat.

$2.99. Darielle Low Carb Pasta (One 12 oz. bag). Most low-carb pastas have a dark color and cook up slightly, shall we say, chewy! This is the best tasting, best texture of low-carb pasta yet! At 10 net carbs per serving (after deducting fiber) these high protein, all-natural, high-fiber, cholesterol-free and GMO-free pastas are simply EXCELLENT!

$3.99. Keto Pastas (One box- 8 oz. [elbows]

- 5 oz. [Mac & Cheese]). (The Elbows are slightly higher in price due to larger box size.) Mix the delicious, soft elbow noodles with your favorite low-carb sauce and you have a new favorite! And, imagine those noodles in a sea of creamy rich Cheddar cheese! That's Keto Mac & Cheese! And all this with just 7 grams of carbs and 22 grams of protein! It includes a packet of Vermont Cheddar cheese mix!

$4.99. Keto Spaghetti (One 8 oz. box)Delicious Semolina taste and texture! 5 grams of effective carbs per serving! Net weight - 8 oz. (226 g) - 6 servings; contains 5 grams of effective carbs per serving.

$16.95. Low Carb Chef Low Carb Pizza Kit (One complete kit - net weight 3 lbs.) The Low Carb Chef Pizza Kit contains sauce, bags of crust mix and pizza seasoning, with complete instructions, enough to make four full pizzas! Each box is a complete kit, just add your own cheeses, toppings and you are all set! The Low Carb Chef has engineered this kit to keep the carbs low, but the taste high! Each plain cheese slice comes in at only FOUR effective carbs!

$7.95. LowCarbolicious Low Carb Pizza Kit (One packet - makes one approx. 12" pizza, with an ECC of just 25 carbs for the entire pizza, and a whopping 54 grams of protein!

$6.49. Pastalia Fettucini (One 9 oz. bag). Pastalia Fettucini is rich with isoflavone enriched soy protein and offers a great alternative to high carb pasta! With NO cholesterol, only .3 of one gram of sugar, 1.5 grams of fat and an amazing 30 grams of protein, it is amazing!

$1.99. Biochem Strive Bars (One 2.1 oz. bar) These new bars are BIG ... no really ... BIG! And, they are crunchy as well! They are about 3/4 of an inch thick by 4 inches long! With only 3 impact carbs per bar (carbs that actually effect blood sugar levels), they are great for low-carbers, hypoglycemics and diabetics!

$22.69. Biochem Strive Bars (One box of 12 - 2.1 oz. bars).

$1.29. Designer Whey SlimWhey Protein Bars (1 - 1.06 oz. - 30 g bar). You get 9 grams of healthy whey protein per bar and only 2 (to 3, depending on flavor) impact carbs! They contain ZERO trans fats.

$17.85. Designer Whey SlimWhey Protein Bars (BOX of 15 - 1.06 oz. - 30 g bars).

$1.89. Doctor's CarbRite Diet Bars (One 2 oz. bar) These bars have a new name (they were called Doctor's Diet LowCarb Bars,) and two new flavors — and the Raspberry Chocolate Truffle contains Phaseolamin Carb Blocker!!! The Chocolate Banana is a new flavor as well, When it comes to taste, moistness and freshness, the Doctor's Diet Bars were voted No. 1 in national taste tests comparing low-carbohydrate bars!

$1.89. Think Thin! Low Carb Diet Bars (One 2.1 oz. bar) Think Products says about these bars: With only 3 grams of carbohydrates, sugar-free, wheat- and gluten-free, it fits in perfectly with a low-carb diet program. Think Thin can be a meal replacement when you are on the go or a quick snack in between healthy meals.

$17.95. Think Thin! Low Carb Diet Bars (One box of 10 - 2.1 oz. bars).

$2.69. Alpine Aire Foods Low Carb Instant Soups (One 1 oz. canister) One thing that we have had to forgo as proponents of the low-carb lifestyle is instant foods! So many are high in carbs, but they are also high in convenience! If only there were low-carb instant foods! Well, now there are! These soups are so simple to use! You just add hot water and boom! Instant low-carb, soup! They are four to six impact carbs depending on flavor and they come in six great flavors.

$4.99. LC Homestyles Microwaveable Meals (One 12 oz. box - 340 g) For a long time, people have asked for microwave-ready meals for low-carbers! Now they are here! LC Homestyles has a true winner with their Microwave Ready Meals for Low Carbers! It's crafted from a homemade recipe and uses only the best ingredients! Pop it in your microwave, and it is ready in minutes!

$3.99. Walden Farms Individual Salad Dressing Packets (One box of 6 - 1 oz. packets) These amazing individually portioned packets of salad dressing are the Holy Grail of any dieter! They are carbohydrate-free, fat-free, calorie-free, cholesterol-free and sugar-free... and taste GREAT! Try any (or all) of the five great flavors! Each flavor comes in a box of six individual-serving packets.

$5.89. Atkins Syrups (One 12 oz. Bottle) You can make low-carb dishes, but have you ever had a hankering for some syrups to add flavor to those dishes? Well, Atkins Nutritionals now has great ZERO CARB flavored syrups that you can use! Sweetened with Splenda, these great syrups will help you be creative in the kitchen, and stay really low in carbs! Use it in coffees, teas, make Atkins sodas (use one part syrup to 6 parts of soda water)! Imagine the uses! Rich tasting and ZERO CARBS!

$1.59. Atkins Quick Quisine Condiments (1 - 10 fl. oz. bottle) (1 gram of impact carbs per serving!) Atkins Quick Quisine Condiments allow us to flavor our low-carb foods with yummy flavorings like: Teriyaki, Barbecue, "Ketch-A-Tomato" and more!

$1.99. Atkins Quick Quisine Salad Dressings (1 - 10 fl. oz. bottle) (1 gram of impact carbs per serving!) Atkins Quick Quisine Salad Dressings give the low-carber a choice when it comes to salad dressings! Instead of JUST oil and vinegar, you can now have: Country French, Lemon Poppyseed, Mustard or Creamy Ranch! All sweetened with Splenda and ready to accent your salad!

$1.29. Drew's All Natural Salad Dressings and Marinades (1 - 12 oz. bottle) (Nine with ZERO Carbs... all VERY low carb!) Eleven varieties. GMO-Free! Many contain no added sweeteners, are dairy-free, low in sodium and wheat- and gluten-free!

$2.69. Flavour Creations Coffee Flavorings
(One dispenser [approx. 48 servings]) Flavour
Creations Coffee Flavorings add spice (literally)
to your morning coffee! They can also be used
for tea, flavoring in cooking and more! Zero
calorie and very low-carb (less than one per
serving!) You get 48 servings per dispenser!
Choose between these exciting flavors: Dutch
Chocolate, Cinnamon Pecan, French Vanilla,
English Toffee, Hazelnut, Irish Creme, Almond
Amaretto, White Chocolate or Raspberry.

**$1.47. Maple Grove Farm's Low Carb,
Sugar-Free Dressings** (1 - 8 oz. bottle) (Only
one impact carb!) Maple Grove Farms of
Vermont make excellent sugar-free, low-carb
dressings — and we have them! Sweetened with
Splenda, these great dressings are a real treat!
Available in Bacon Vinaigrette, Dijon and
Italian Balsamic!

$5.99. DeBoer Sugar-Free Twist (One 14
oz. jar) These spreads can turn a lowly piece of
low-carb bread into a sweet treat! And they can
turn the Cheeters Diet Treats Muffins
Chocolate Muffins into cupcakes! They have
just 2.2 grams of carbs per serving (2 tablespoons)!

$5.49. Keto Low Carb Fruit Spreads (One 10 oz. jar) Keto Low Carb Fruit Spreads contain only 2 grams of carbohydrates per serving! (1 tablespoon per serving, 17 servings per jar.) These new, luscious, low-carb Fruit Spreads are imported from clean, green New Zealand! All of the delicious flavors are lovingly hand-crafted in small, kettle-stirred batches. Hand-picked ripe and plump native fruits are chopped and crushed into thick, sucralose-sweetened low-carb syrup!

$0.99. Racquet Low Carb Dips (1 - 8.5 tub) Racquet's Low Carb Dips are excellent! All natural, no cholesterol, no preservatives and a great source of calcium! One to two impact carbs per serving depending on flavor!

$6.50. Rosie's Gold Low Carb Apple Butter (One 11 oz. jar) This is an ol' Southern favorite! Apple Butter! But, isn't apple butter WAY too high in carbs? Well, normally, YES! But bless the folks at Rosie's Gold ... they have made apple butter for those of us living the low-carb lifestyle! They exchange the sugars for polyols. And they have made a great apple butter that comes in at 2 net carbs per serving! Sweet and tasty like your Grandmamma made!

$3.99. Walden Farms ZERO Carb Dips (1 - 12 oz. [340g] jar). With these great dips, you can enjoy so many things ... (like fresh, ripe strawberries!) dipped in chocolate or marshmallow!

$9.99. Now Foods Liquid Stevia Extract (One 2 oz. bottle). It is just pure, natural Stevia Extract, but in a liquid! *Stevia Rebaudiana* is a plant found in South America, where the natives have been using it for over a thousand years to safely sweeten their foods.

$9.95. Now Stevia Balance (One box of 100 packets - 3.5 oz. per box). Stevia is great! But, it can be hard to measure and use since it is 300 times sweeter than sugar! What if you could use stevia as easily as sugar? What if it came in convenient packets? And, what if it didn't contain a lot of fillers that add a lot of carbs, like maltodextrin, as some stevia packets have? Well, it is here!

$8.99. Low Carb Success Erythritol (One 1 lb. packet - approx. 30 servings). Sugar alcohols, or polyols, are amazing things! They aren't actually sugar, nor are they alcohols, but they are sweet! Most polyols end in "ol," like Maltitol, Mannitol and Erythritol. Erythritol is different in several ways, it is NOT as sweet as sugar, it is cooler to the taste buds, it has a refreshingly cool taste ... but no aftertaste.

$6.99, Nutragenics Fiberfit Concentrated Soluble Fiber (One 4 oz. bottle). Fiber is an essential part of any diet. It helps keep your digestive system healthy and regular. When following a low-carb lifestyle, some sources of fiber are curtailed. Nutragenics Fiberfit Concentrated Soluble Fiber can be added to beverages and used in cooking to add in fiber, while adding a smooth, sweet taste! Fiberfit has 1 gram of carbohydrate, but 1 gram of fiber per serving.

$4.99. Perfect Sweet Xylitol Sweetener (One 8 oz. [227 gram] canister) Perfect Sweet Xylitol tastes as sweet as sugar and the sweetness remains in your mouth (like sugar!) It measures just like sugar and you can cook with it! It also helps reduce development of dental caries (cavities.) It is low calorie — only 2.4 calories/gram (sugar is 4.0 calories/gram). And amazingly, it has a glycemic index of 7 (while sugar has a glycemic index of 100!)

$20.99. Splenda. Granular (One box of 700 Packets - 1.54 lbs. per box).

$2.99. Steel's Honey Flavor Nature Sweet

Sweetener (1 - 64 oz. jar). (ZERO grams of impact carbs per serving!) Steel's has done it again! Now they have a sweet Honey Replacement! You heard right! Some folks just love honey on their toast, but it is full of sugar carbs! Not this "honey!" It is Steel's Nature Sweet Sweetener in "Honey Flavor!" And with 6 grams of total carbs, of which 6 grams are Maltitol, that is a total of ZERO impact carbs!

$19.99. Steel's Nature Sweet Maltitol Sweeteners (One 2 lb. bag - approx. 302 servings). Folks love to develop their own low-carb, sugar-free recipes! The problem has been to have a sweetener that measures like sugar AND that will caramelize like sugar! Steel's Nature Sweet Sweeteners do JUST THAT! Now you can make those yummy treats that you have been dreaming of ... so stop dreaming and start baking! Steel's Sweeteners come in big 2 lb. bags of Brown Sugar, Powdered and Crystal versions!

There you have it. And don't forget: There are still 1,199,999 Web sites to check out in that same Google search.

Many of these foods are available at well-stocked supermarkets, or in specialty stores in your own neighborhood. And they are only a sampling of the thousands of products in the marketplace, with more companies climbing onto the low-carb bandwagon every week.

ConAgra Foods, for example, now offers special low-carb dinners, complete entrees, for those who don't have the time to shop and cook. Some of their offerings include:

- Beef Pot Roast, with green beans and red peppers.
- Slow Roasted Beef Tips, with mushroom sauce, broccoli and carrots.
- Hearty Meat Loaf, with sauce, broccoli and cauliflower, topped with cheddar cheese.
- Salisbury Steak, with mushroom sauce, green beans and carrots.
- Roasted Turkey Breast, with sauce, green beans and carrots.
- Oven Roasted Turkey, with creamy mushroom sauce, brussels sprouts, red peppers and celery.
- Three Meat Alfredo, with chicken breast, alfredo sauce, ham and bacon with broccoli.
- Italian Sausage Scramble-Breakfast, with eggs, marinara sauce, vegetables and cheese.
- Sausage, Beef & Bacon Scramble-Breakfast, with eggs, country gravy, green beans, cheese and mushrooms.

CHAPTER 15

FIND IT ONLINE

L ittle did the developers of the first personal computers back in the '70s realize their machines would become a major force in helping Americans lose weight 30 years later. But that's what is happening, reports the Calorie Control Council.

"With almost two-thirds of Americans overweight, dieting is top of the mind, " the council reports. "And one of the latest trends in dieting is the use of Web-based resources and tools for weight loss. Weight-conscious people are increasingly utilizing online resources to guide and assist their weight-loss efforts."

One of those resources is the Council's own Web site, www.caloriecontrol.org. Though it doesn't emphasize low-carb dieting, it does offer a computer-driven calculator that will let you learn your Body Mass Index (BMI), a more accurate measure of fat-to-muscle ratio, and another that will help you determine how many calories you must cut from your personal diet to lose weight.

A study at Brown University Medical School shows that weight-loss programs on the Internet can hep people lose weight.

Diet on the Web is totally private; no gawkers or more successful dieters to sneer at you in a class. And for those with busy lives filled with careers and family, you can't beat the Internet for convenience; you can use it whenever you have a few minutes free.

"The advantage of online dieting is that it offers convenience and complete privacy," says John Foreyt, a leading obesity researcher with Baylor College of Medicine and scientific advisory board member for CaloriesCount.com — a Web site dedicated to teaching and helping consumers achieve and maintain a healthy weight for life.

Here are just a few guidelines for selecting a responsible Internet weight-loss program, recommended by the Calorie Control Council:

● It should not promise or guarantee a specific weight loss in a predetermined time-frame (such as "Lose 20 lbs. in four weeks!").

● It should not sell mailing lists or other information to third-party vendors.

● It should promote healthy eating and exercise habits that can be maintained long-term.

● It should offer access and support from qualified dietitians or other health professionals.

● It should incorporate exercise.

But the very best consumer Internet site for low-carb dieters is, in my humble opinion, www.lowcarbluxury.com.

At lowcarbluxury.com, you'll find links to scores of other Web sites that offer a treasure trove of information useful to those practicing the low-carb lifestyle.

These are a few, with a description of each:

❑ **Carbohydrate Awareness Council:** The Carbohydrate Awareness Council is committed to encouraging health and well-being through controlled-carbohydrate nutrition. Their guiding principles are built on a foundation of scientific-evidence, honesty and service.

❑ **Low-Carb Consumers League:** The Low-Carb League is a nonprofit association dedicated to establishing and adopting scientifically based nutritional, manufacturing, testing and marketing standards on behalf of low-carb consumers.

❑ **Truly Low Carb.** Karen Rysavy's fun and sassy site devoted to her total passion of low-carbing. A visit to Karen's site is fun as well as educational, and she'll share a rant or two with you at the same time! Karen has published a cookbook as well (*Truly Low Carb Cooking*) that can be purchased at the site.

❑ **Laura Richard's Low Carb Success**. Author of the book of the same name, Laura offers her personal story, insights and tips. Plus tons of links.

❑ **The USDA's Searchable Nutritional Database**. A quick search will tell you what the official nutritional data is for most "base" foods (non-commercially packaged foods). Enter key-words to locate item(s) of interest.

You can reach all of these sites by clicking on their links at lowcarbluxury.com. And while you're there, you can check out the **FREE** *Low Carb Luxury Online* magazine and the wealth of low-carb recipes you can add to those in this book to develop your own personal menu plans.

These are a few other important Web sites:

❑ www.atkins.com. The official Web site of the Atkins organization, where you could spend hours reading the helpful information available, including tips on low-carb eating, recipes, research results and more.

❑ www.zonediet.com. This is Barry Sears' personal Web site. It, too, contains a wealth of information and links to his 9 books on The Zone as well as to other Web sites.

❑ www.fatflush.com. Ann Louise Gittleman, Ph.D., C.N.S., offers helpful advice including a FREE personal diet profile, information on her best-selling book, recipes and a wealth of support information for dieters. You can get more information, including a copy of the *Fat Flush Plan* and Kit, at www.fatflush.com, visited now by some 700,000 people a day, she says, or by calling 1-800-888-4353.

❑ www.southbeachdiet.com, where Arthur Agatston, M.D., provides support for dieters, helpful articles, tips of low-carb products and pointers to other diet books.

❑ www.carbohydrateaddicts.com. Here, Drs. Richard and Rachel Heller, M.D., authors of *The Carbohydrate Addicts Diet*, offer a quiz that will tell you whether YOU are addicted to carbohydrates, and other useful information.

❑ www.eatprotein.com. Drs. Michael and Mary Dan Eades provide updates on their best-selling book, *Protein Power*, the latest developments in research, recipes and an online chat group for those in need of support.

❑ dreamfieldsfoods.com. Where you will find more recipes for delicious low-carb pasta dishes.

INDEX

A

Agatston, Arthur,
    M.D. **53-58**, 331
Alcohol 21
American Dietetic
    Association 10
American Heart
    Association Diet 27
*American Journal of
    Nutrition*, 35
American Snack Food
    Association 142
Annie's Edibles 39
Arthur, Wendy, M.D.
    12
Atkins Diet 13, 16,
    19, 24, **25-36**, 54,
    58, 149
Atkins, Robert, M.D.
    11, **25-36**

B

Baylor College of
    Medicine 328
Beaty, Neil 270
Body Mass Index 328
Breast cancer 12
Brolus, Doug 159-160

Brown University
    Medical School 328
Bullock, Sandra 39

C

Calorie Control
    Council 9, 327, 328
*Cancer Epidemiology,
    Biomarkers and
    Prevention* 12
Carb counter 17, 24,
    150, **161-270**
Carbohydrate
    Awareness Council
    329
Clayton College 12

D

Duke University 11,
    27

E

Eades, Drs. Michael
    and Mary Dan 331
Elliott, David James
    40
Exercise 16, 60, **152-
    161**

F

Fat Flush Plan 13, 16, **43-53**, 58, 331
Long-life cocktail 45, 46
Foreyt, John 328

G

Gittleman, Ann Louise, Ph.D., C.N.S 13, **43-53**, 331

H

Harvard School of Public Health 12
Heller, Drs. Richard and Rachel, M.D. 331

I

Internet 17, 22, 61, **327-332**

J

Journal of the American Medical Association 147

K

Ketosis 31-32

L

LaLanne, Jack 159
Laura Richard's Low Carb Success 330
Los Angeles Farm 40
Low Carb Luxury 270-276
  Product Spotlight 270-275
Low-Carb Consumers League 329
Low-carb food products 17, 22, 60, **270-327**

M

M.I.T. 36
Mastroianni, Annalisa 39, 40

N

National Health and Nutrition Examination Survey 10

National Institutes of Health 22

Night-eating syndrome 146-147

Nutrition Facts panel 22

P

Parton, Dolly 39

Pritikin Longevity Center 44

Protein Power 331

R

Ray, Lisa 40

Recipes 17, 59, **80-142**

BEEF 113-122

Asian Beef Salad 120-121

Burgundy Beef & Vegetable Stew 113-114

Grilled Beef Eye Round Steaks with Garlic-Yogurt Marinade 115-116

Grilled Beef Sirloin & Farmers

Market Skewers 114-115

Grilled T-Bone Steaks With Barbecue Rub 116-117

Lemon-Herb Beef Pot Roast 117-118

Mediterranean Braised Beef 121-122

Pepper-Rubbed Shoulder Center Steak 118-119

Peppery Beef Tri-Tip with Skewered Vegetables 119-120

CHICKEN 99-107

Cajun Chicken Breasts 102-103

Chicken and Spinach Medley 101-102

Grilled Chicken Breasts With Spicy Salsa 103-104

Healthful Chicken Casserole 99-100

Quick Coriander Chicken Breasts 104-105

Spanish Olive Chicken 105-106

Stir-Fry Chicken With Vegetables 100-101

Vietnamese Chicken in Tomato Sauce 106-107

EGGS 95-99

Cauliflower Frittata 97-99

Italian Tidbits 96-97

Quiche Florentine 95-96

Scrambled or fried 99

FAVORITES 132-142

Chicken Provencal 136

Chicken Scallopini 135-136

Chinese Beef and Vegetables 139-140

Enriched Hamburger With Farm-fresh Grilled Vegetables 138-139

Grilled or Broiled Steak — a traditional American treat 138

Grilled Pork Chops With Cheese and Garlic Cauliflower 140

Pineapple Grilled Salmon 134-135

Sea and Farm Medley 133-134

Seafood Stew 132-133

Shish Kebab 137-138

LAMB 122-125

Celebration Leg of Lamb 124-125

Rosemary Grilled Lamb Loin Chops with Cranberry and Peppered Apple Relish 123

PASTA 107-112

Baked Penne Pasta with Tomatoes and Mozzarella 107-108

Elbow Macaroni Salad 111

Linguine Puttanesca 108-109

Southwest Pasta Salad 110-111

Spaghetti with Prosciutto and Asparagus 109-110

Thai-Style Penne 112-113

PORK 80-94

Caribbean-style Pork Rib Chops 85-86

Carolina Country Style Ribs 86-87

Grilled Chimichurri Pork Roast 81-82

Grilled Honey-Soy Pork Steaks 87-88

Grilled Leg of Pork 83-84

Herbed Butterfly Pork Chops 80

Italian Pork Spiedini 93-94

Jerk Pork Chops 84-85

Lean Homemade Breakfast Sausage 82-83

Masitas de Cerdo 92

North Beach Pork Bocconcini 89-90

Peppered Pork Tenderloin 80-81

Quick-Cured Pork Loin 83

Quick-Mix Breakfast Sausage 94-95

Raleigh-Durham Pork Barbecue 91

Roasted Pork Tenderloin with Oregano-Coriander Rub 92-93

Sausage Sprout Omelet 88-89

Sweet & Sour Pork
    Meatballs 90-91
SEAFOOD 125-132
Baked Oysters
    Appetizer 128
Broccoli and
    Mushroom
    Scallops 126-127
Garlic Skewered
    Shrimp 125-126
Oyster Salad 130-131
Shrimp Salad-
    Southern Style
    131-132
Shrimp Scampi 127
Tuna Salad and
    Shrimp 128-129
**Restaurants/Eating
out 148-152**
Ruffner, Lora, R.N.
    270
Rysavy, Karen 329

S

Sample menu plans
    17, 55, 59, 63-80
Just For Men 70-76
Just for Woman 63-
    70

Schneider Children's
    Hospital 31
Schwarzenegger,
    Arnold 159
Sears, Barry, Ph.D.
    36-43, 63, 66-67,
    147, 330
Snacking 17, 60, **142-
148**
Zone Snacks 76-77
South Beach Diet 14,
    16, **53-58**
Stunkard, Albert,
    M.D. 147

T

*The Carbohydrate
    Addicts Diet* 331
**The Ultimate Low-
    Carb Plan** 12, 14-17,
    24, **58-63**, 149
Truly Low Carb 329
*Truly Low Carb
    Cooking* 330

U

U.S. Department of
    Agriculture 17, 61,
    161-270, 330

Food and Nutrition
    Service 17, 61, 161-
    270
University of Miami 53
University of
    Pennsylvania 11, 27,
    147

W

Water 78-79
Westman, Eric, Dr. 27
www.atkins.com 330
www.caloriecontrol.
    org 327
www.caloriescount.
    com 328
www.carb-counter.org
    161
www.carbohydrate
    addicts.com 331
www.carbsmart.com
    276
www.dreamfields
    foods.com 331
www.eatprotein.com
    331
www.fatflush.com 331
www.low-carb.com
    276

www.lowcarbdieters.
    com 276
www.lowcarbluxury.
    com 276, 329, 330
www.lowcarbnexus.
    com 276
www.nal.usda.gov/
    fnic 161
www.southbeachdiet.
    com 331
www.zonediet.com
    330

Y

Yo-yo Syndrome 10,
    18, 59

Z

Zone Diet 14, 16, 35,
    36-43, 54, 58, 63,
    147, 331
    Eye-and-palm
        method 41